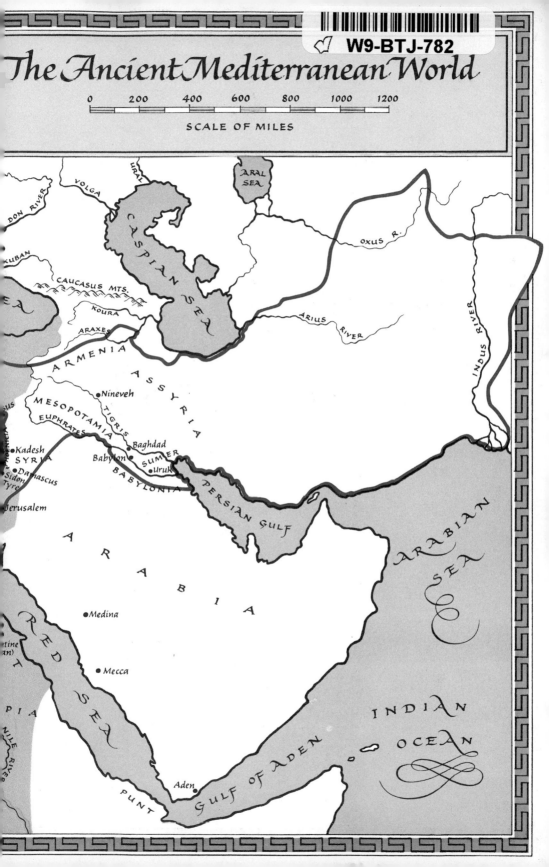

The Ancient Mediterranean World

0   200   400   600   800   1000   1200

SCALE OF MILES

Other books by Alexander Eliot:

Proud Youth   (1953)

Three Hundred Years of American Painting (1957)

Sight and Insight   (1959)

A Personal Adventure

into the Sources of Our Life and Legend

by

ALEXANDER ELIOT

With Photographs by Jane Winslow Eliot

SIMON AND SCHUSTER

NEW YORK   1962

EARTH,

AIR,

FIRE

AND

WATER

A portion of "River Wrestler" originally appeared in Sports Illustrated *under the title "The Water Tamer."*

A portion of "The Earthborn Art" (pages 37-48) originally appeared in Sports Illustrated *under the title "Men Like Gods."*

A portion of "Death and a Pharaoh" originally appeared in Life *magazine under the title "World of Ramses II."*

A portion of "Some Dark Roots of Joy" originally appeared in the Saturday Evening Post *under the title "The Sense of Joy."*

A portion of "The Earthborn Art" (pages 48-60) originally appeared in Life International *under the title "The Wine and the Marble."*

A portion of "One Glass of Raki" originally appeared in Life International *under the title "Istanbul."*

"Wonder on Parnassus" will appear in the Saturday Evening Post.

A portion of "Some Dark Roots of Joy" appeared in Harper's Bazaar *under the title "Children of the Storm."*

A portion of "The Search Without a Stop" appeared in Harper's Bazaar *under the title "Who Is Barbarous?"*

The author thanks the following for permission to reprint the material listed below:

Chappell and Co., Inc., for the lines from "It Ain't Necessarily So" by Ira Gershwin from Porgy and Bess by George and Ira Gershwin, copyright 1935 by Gershwin Publishing Corporation, New York, N. Y. Sole selling agent: Chappell and Co., Inc. By special permission of the publisher.

The Clarendon Press, Oxford, for the translations by George Allen, A. J. Butler, Jack Lindsay, and Gilbert Murray from The Oxford Book of Greek Verse in Translation. Reprinted by permission of the Clarendon Press, Oxford.

The John Day Company, Inc., for the selection from Monkey by Wu Chen-En, translated by Arthur Waley. Reprinted by permission of The John Day Company, Inc., publisher.

Holt, Rinehart and Winston, Inc., for the lines from "Caboose Thoughts" from Cornhuskers by Carl Sandburg, copyright 1918 by Holt, Rinehart and Winston, Inc., copyright renewed 1946 by Carl Sandburg. Reprinted by permission of Holt, Rinehart and Winston, Inc.; for the lines from "A Peck of Gold" from Complete Poems of Robert Frost, copyright 1928 by Holt, Rinehart and Winston, Inc., copyright renewed © 1956 by Robert Frost. Reprinted by permission of Holt, Rinehart and Winston, Inc.

Indiana University Press for the selection from Ovid's Metamorphoses, translated by Rolfe Humphries. Reprinted by permission of Indiana University Press.

Robert Lax for the use of his untitled poem on page 33.

The Macmillan Company for the selection from Collected Poems by Edwin Arlington Robinson, copyright 1925 by Edwin Arlington Robinson, copyright 1952 by Ruth Nivison and Barbara Holt; for the selection from the introduction to The Way and Its Power by Arthur Waley; for the lines from Collected Poems by William Butler Yeats, copyright 1928 by The Macmillan Company, copyright © 1956 by Bertha Georgie Yeats. Reprinted with permission of the Macmillan Company.

Penguin Books, Ltd., for the four selections from The Epic of Gilgamesh, translated by N. K. Sandars; for the passage from Tristan, translated by A. T. Hatto. Reprinted by permission of Penguin Books, Ltd., publishers.

The World Publishing Company for the selection from The Greek Experience by C. M. Bowra. Copyright © 1957 by C. M. Bowra. Reprinted by permission of The World Publishing Company.

DEDICATION

If a man's life may be compared to an arrow's flight
His father and mother are the bow and the bowstring.

Though a man's work resemble an arrow's passing whir
Yet he honors his parents and the unknown archer too.

ACKNOWLEDGMENTS

The author is grateful to the Solomon R. Guggenheim Memorial Foundation and the America-Israel Cultural Foundation, whose fellowships enabled him to follow his delight in eastern Mediterranean lands. He owes a companionable debt to many writers, ancient and modern, especially those quoted herein. Fragments of the work in progress were published by Life *and* Life International, *the* Saturday Evening Post, Sports Illustrated *and* Harper's Bazaar, *and thanks go to the editors of these magazines. Finally, friends of all kinds and conditions are to be thanked for having dealt themselves into the work, materially, emotionally and intellectually. Among them are the Platonist Huntington Cairns, the Hellenist Alkiviadis Kalapothakis, the antiquarian Karl Katz, the philhellene James A. Linen, the inventor Michael Lavelle, the surgeon Wilbur J. Gould, the economist Leo Model, the painters Henry Koerner and James N. Rosenberg, the collator Rita Langford and the editor Henry Simon.*

CONTENTS

PROLOGUE

What will you do, Alex, what will you do when there are no more museums?

That strange question changed my life completely, and it led to my writing this. So I will begin by telling how the question came to be asked. At the time I was on leave from a national magazine which I served as art editor. The post was influential, near the center of the cultural whirl. I loved that glittering carousel and I had no intention of stepping down from it. Then came a flying trip to Greece, just to look at some sculpture. My wife and I spent a day at Delphi—an overwhelming day because Delphi is sculpture from no human hand. And that night, in dream, I heard a strong voice calling me by name, asking the question. Until then, art had been my chief delight. To me it seemed a sort of stained-glass window through which the light of truth poured confusing treasure. My profession as I saw it was to interpret that dazzle upon the air. Or, in plainer language, it was to find the meanings in art. A not unpleasant way to spend one's working life! But—*What will you do when there are no more museums?*

Awakening at once I lay very still, thinking over the question. It made no sense if taken literally, but as an abstract proposition it did. I translated it in less oracular terms this way: "Just suppose, Alex Eliot, that there were no more museums, no more works of art for you to enjoy and interpret. Then what would you do with your life?" And the first answer I found went something like this: "Even with no art to look at, I could still be searching for meanings. Because the light of truth would still be there, even without the stained glass." Or would it? Is truth really an all-embracing light? Like the light of human reason, perhaps! I could not think so now. So soon after my dream, I could not believe such a thing. I closed my eyes again, thinking that truth perhaps is something one touches, or that touches one, in the dark—for good or ill. But in the dawn, what of truth? Must it not be something drawn out of nature and shaped anew for recognition's sake, for daylight knowing? I swung my feet out of bed, thinking: art, science, mathematics? May not truth which comes as a dream in the night appear by day as a refinement of fact? I stood now at the window of our hotel room, breathing the sharp dark air. This window was no work of art, to be sure, yet it could serve as the nearest sample of human, intellectual and technical refinement. Beyond it I saw a single treetop, dark against the dawn.

This tree seemed standing up to peer at me, or through me, and through the whole hotel. The tree stood clothed in the dark breathing mantle of truth, and peered right through me. The hotel itself, by way of contrast, withered away to the condition of dry, fragile fact. And I to myself appeared unusually naked and forlorn; hardly better than a fact myself: a bit of dust off the streets of New York, encapsulated, vain. My feet were cold.

Some hours later, at the Athens airport, I remarked to my wife, "We're coming back here to live." It was the decision of a moment, nonrational and yet final. We never thought of reversing it, then or later. I am aware that this will strike some people as being irresponsible, the more so since our young children were involved. But there it is. I extricated myself from my job and tidied up my affairs as best I could. Meanwhile I plunged into the study of scientific and philosophic theory. This development naturally startled certain of my friends. "How can you care about such things, let alone understand them?" was a question frequently asked. And I could only reply that all of us do care about and understand such things. In fact science and philosophy are on everybody's lips nowadays. Yet too often we care with averted eyes, and understand what is not there.

My own modest findings were published in an essay called "The Sense of Truth"—which concluded with the flat statement that "truth is nature, and nature is experience." I felt that the ancient Greeks had been on to this idea, not as something to preach but as a dark, single background to the rigors and the glories of their world. Well, as an indirect result of this essay, certain fellowships were offered me "for studies of Greece and the Near East as spiritual homelands of the West." So I happily bundled my family aboard a freighter headed for our new home. Like everyone who sails from his native land to settle elsewhere, I was filled with tender thoughts and a shy sort of pride in our common heritage. We do belong, I thought, to a profoundly generous and moral society, and we are healthily self-critical besides. Yet as a people we tend to be unnatural in one respect: we lack joy. Keeping alive is no problem for most Americans, but meanwhile living itself becomes little better than a hobby. Was this too rough an opinion? Naturally I included myself among the hobbyists, though I confess that the personal application came as quite a shock to me. There seems to be some hidden law of compensation which balances out our surfeit of security, our massed pleasures. Yet surely the main purpose of living is not to keep the glum beast in us alive and well and tamed with fond affection. It is to enjoy reality.

My fellowships called for a good deal of travel in eastern Mediterranean lands, and for this I made Herodotus my model. The ancient historian went to see the truth of things in person and to question the best authorities alive. One amiable weakness of his I will try to adopt: he could not resist telling a good anecdote or story in context. Also he dared to mingle myths, arts and sciences with history—and I will do the same. One thing I cannot emulate, however, is Herodotus' classic calm. I hope this book will provide some insights into the ancient world as well as our own, and possibly some experience of the author's heart.

Now I have brought my family to rest in a little house upon the shoulder of Mount Pentelikon. Here our back gate swings wide to piney, pastoral realm. The clear light, the clear air bless our eyes and breath. We have begun a garden. And I have set my mind to writing "Earth, Air, Fire and Water." Why call it that? Or why trouble about the title at all? Authors waste a lot of time worrying about titles, which the publishers then change. Yet this one will have to stand, because it embodies my whole concept of nature as experience. Of course from any one person's viewpoint, nature is a matter of personal experience, but I mean experience in a larger sense. What is the totality of nature? Old-fashioned scientists reply with a list of chemical—objective—"elements." And they name a hundred and more varieties of these. But there is more to nature than chemistry: for instance, conscious life. There still exists the ancient abyss between chemistry and consciousness, between atoms and thoughts; let's face the fact. The chemical elements cannot bridge it. Yet in a sense the four elements of classical philosophy can and do. Earth, Air, Fire and Water are what bridge the abyss. Because these four alone belong both to the physical world and to the world of human feeling. They exist in everything we know directly. A very particular grouping of these four, something unique perhaps, is what makes up our planet and ourselves. Here are the wellsprings of human being, both inside and out. But this point has never, to my knowledge, been made before. The ancient Greeks had no need to state what must have seemed self-evident to them. Modern thinkers, on the other hand, tend to consider "objective" and "subjective" reality as poles apart. So the elemental bridge between the two has remained invisible to them. Scientifically considered, the classic four elements are of course mere conglomerates, with no specific atomic weights. But humanly considered, they are, I repeat, everything to us.

Would any human being, given a clear choice in the matter, prefer a whining sound to heavenly music? For the material-minded and machine-bound man, nature just whines like an infinite swarm of atoms. Whereas to the few individuals who seriously enjoy her, she sings. Earth, Air, Fire and Water weave the song of life. They make pleasant the solitudes of Mount Pentelikon; they are moving in the woods at my back as I write, and lifting the birds of this clearing. They form conscious and creative powers at a breath. They are woven in the cities that we build by the sea, in the arts of our own bodies. They are pharaonic ritual, Greek sculpture, what you will. They are Heracles, Aphrodite, this whole sacred world—given to us.

PART ONE

EARTH

Olympia, the sacred precinct, where men strove
to act like gods.

Archaic Greek sculpture, the Youth of Melos:
". . . with feet so light to pass through life."

SOME DARK ROOTS OF JOY

THE OTHER NIGHT I dreamed myself in the midst of a brawl, and I behaved accordingly. Soon tremendous thunders awakened me; what a relief! I lay flat on my back. But the whole house was shaking like a rattle. Our fox-fur blanket was already crusted white with hailstones. Instead of shutting the window, I moved over like a sensible person and let the storm have most of our bed. Such violent tempests are a rarity in Greece, too good to miss. The whole air was one furious cloud: streaming, coiling, spitting, split with intermittent fires. The lightning bursts let me see my garden pelted to death with fistfuls of icy thick hail. White chrysanthemums, white petunias, white bitter-daphne, even white geraniums dancing, sprawling and disintegrating.

Beyond the garden, all Mount Pentelikon rocked and shone, like a boulder in a waterfall. The peak stood wreathed in lightnings. Its NATO radar saucers pricked up as if in obedience to the hoarse booming voice of Zeus, bright and dark. I thought of the technicians blinking at their stations, shaken and blistered with blips. In the heaving land between our house and the crest, thousands of wild things live. I wondered how they were feeling.

The bushes, full of songbirds at this season, cracking, breaking and exploding like clustered shotguns. The popeyed frogs, hopping, with throbbing heads. The vixen loping home to her cubs, her brush held straight out and prickling with electricity. The tortoises grinning in their brown bone houses, hearing the hail bounce off. The homeless dogs assembling on the porch of a padlocked hunting lodge, their ears laid back and muzzles trembling, tails between their legs, each one yearning for a master. The sluggish viper coming half-awake to feel the shaking of his hide-out, swelling up and writhing briefly; a knot made and untied again as he dozes off to dream of summer noons. The creaking wreck of a hollow tree crashing down, and inside it an owl's yellow eyes, round with no astonishment. The clever field mice tweeting and preening in their dry burrows, suddenly flooded out. Insects squeezing under streaming stones, or riding the undersides of torn leaves and knocking branches. The beehives snoring under thunder's kettledrum. A flock of sheep in a hollow, pressed together like one forlorn wet fleece. The sopping sheep dog worriedly nibbling at the corners of the flock, while the shepherd whistles encouragement—between thunderbursts—from the shelter of a soughing, hissing pine.

Every creature lives at the center of its own universe, and trembles when its universe is shaken. Yet at the same time each individual is a part of all creation, of a single, continuous reality.

We call this a paradox, but it is no paradox except in our own minds; it is a fact. Animals feel the fact intensely. Trees and flowers know it right down to their roots. So storms bring ecstasy as well as fear. They can even shake a man straight out of himself.

Three days afterwards the flowers which had writhed so white in the lightning, knocking their soft fragrant heads in ice and slime, started running up new colors. The autumn sun poured down its rich light. To celebrate the break in the weather, my family went off on a picnic. As for me, I stayed home to repair the garden trellises. I was feeling marvelous but lonely, when along came a friend from Athens. Waving a newspaper, he turned in at the gate. "Who wants news?" I thought; but it comes anyhow. The glorious storm had wrought black mourning, the torrents turned to blood, the headlines said. Thousands were homeless, hundreds injured, over forty people dead.

Later my friend blurted out the question on his mind: "Is it fair to ask people to rejoice in the sunrise when what they really see is headlines like these? Natural disasters alternating with the ones we bring on ourselves, things more terrible still! Under these circumstances how can you detach yourself from the world? Is it fair to go searching for a sense of joy?" He was trying to conceal his disapproval, swallowing it back even as he spoke. And I had the gall to tease him with a few lines from Horace: advice which the rustic poet gave to his friend Virgil, in a dark time long ago:

> *Keep the dark flames of death in mind while you may,*
> *And mix a little silliness into your scheming;*
> *Sometimes it's good to be foolish.*

Besides, I said, detachment is impossible. You leave one world only to enter another. God knows there's more to life than what you read in the papers; something more, and so much, much better. "Joy is the thanks we give to God," as Socrates explained. I'm for that. If man's inhumanity to man is hateful, so is the primal sort: inhumanity to oneself. Personally I do feel an obligation to the life that's been given me. There is a kind of call to rejoice.

In silence, my friend arose and strolled about the garden, restlessly prodding the flowers with his cane. Then he wandered back to confront me: "Horace had a full belly! That's why he could afford to be foolish. Even today some of you writers pretend that everything's rosy. And you cloak this pleasant fancy in a semblance of reality. Who can blame you?"

It's the reverse! I exclaimed. Imagination is the cloak. Or the cloak I use, anyhow, to smuggle a little real news into print. Not just disaster-stuff.

Towards sunset we walked along the mountain for a glimpse of distant Marathon. The high slope had on its fall mantle of sparkling moss. Cyclamen gleamed here and there in the crevices. Crows flocked and called above us, homeward bound. The broad bay was a glistening blue-violet, like dusky purple grapes. There is a kind of wine in the sea, as Homer knew. The Greeks called it *plankton:* wandering currents of microscopic diatoms, copepods, comb-jellies, bristly euphausiids, protozoa . . . flecks of the sun submerged. This sacrificial wine runs thickest, of course, in the great oceans. Tests on the North Sea coast have turned up twelve and a half million plant cells along with many thousand marine animals in a single bucket. Strange that nobody can take sea water home. The life dies out of it, as every land-child knows.

That evening, at the bus stop, my friend patted his pocket and groaned: "I forgot my newspaper!"

Never mind, I said. There would be others.

The lights of the oncoming bus raked across his kindly, troubled face: "One last thing; why try to write about the forces of nature? Are you doing it by way of propitiation? They don't listen, you know." As I was searching for an answer, he lightly stepped aboard the bus.

I know propitiation is not possible. As for listening: can anybody say for sure who listens or what listens in this world? All being part of the same song.

The song of the four elements! The next morning I sat idle at my desk, thinking about it. How had I ever found the nerve, I wondered, to begin writing on such a subject? Only a poet could do justice . . . And as if on signal there came shouldering between the pines, into my room, this chant:

Μανάβης!
'Αγκινάρες, καλά 'αγγούρια, κεράσια,
Πατάτες, ντομάτες, κολοκύθια καί φράουλες!
Μανάβης!

It was the vegetable-man, passing by with his donkey cart on his way down to the village. His lungs are bellows of brass: his chant reverberated through the house and re-echoed from the marble peaks of Mount Pentelikon at our back door. If any chant has a claim to immortality, his does. Roughly translated, it runs:

Fruits of Earth!
Artichokes, fine cucumbers, cherries,
Potatoes, tomatoes, squashes and strawberries!
Fruits of Earth!

We all came out at the call, as we do most mornings: our hound to bark at the man, my wife to buy of him, our children to climb up on his patient, sardonic little donkey, and I to enjoy the general commotion under the glistening pines. After a while the vegetable-man went on down the lane, shouting Χαίρετε! to us all. The word means both "hello" and "goodbye" in colloquial Greek. Its actual meaning, however, is *Rejoice!* And thereby hangs a tale . . .

Four hundred and ninety years before the birth of Christ, the Greeks defeated an enormously superior force of invading Persians at Marathon. The news of this almost incredible and world-changing victory was sent back to Athens by a footrunner. He had about twenty-five miles to cover; no doubt he sprinted much of the way. Arriving at the gates of his native city he gasped out one word only: Χαίρετε! *Rejoice!* And he fell dead even as Athens' answering cry—its goodbye to despair and glad hello to a glorious new fate—went up. In that cry was Western civilization born.

Back at my desk after the vegetable-man's departure, I got to wishing that such loud chants as his, such welcomings to the new day, might be heard in my native New England. Also, that more of us could or would carry in our hearts the greeting, *Rejoice!* Everybody criticizes Americans for something or other; I have no special liking for that game. Besides, it would seem a bit unsporting to complain, here on my Greek mountain, of how things are at home. Yet I am haunted by the specter of the Joyless American. So often it happens that in Yankeedom, as Edward Arlington Robinson observed:

> *Joy shivers in the corner where she knits*
> *And Conscience always has the rocking-chair,*
> *Cheerful as when she tortured into fits*
> *The first cat that was ever killed by Care.*

This is not to say that life in America lacks pleasures; no, the country is all too crammed with those, and with "conveniences" to boot. Also it is crowded with psychotics and neurotics—the so-called "walking wounded" victims of profound inner anxiety. There has been much ingenious speculation on the roots of this anxiety. I hold it to stem from a basically sound awareness that pleasure is not joy. Money and fame, for example, bring pleasure merely. Therefore they are not enough. Creative work and love bring joy. So does each new day that dawns for the happy man. But for him without joy, though he be as a king, there is no "new day" at all: no renewal. Sophocles makes this bitter point in his

Antigone. The man without joy, says Sophocles, "is but a breathing corpse. Heap up riches in thy house, if thou wilt. Live in kindly state. Yet, if there be no gladness therein, I would not give the shadow of a vapor for all the rest—compared with joy."

What then is this greatest of all boons, this elixir of life itself? Is it not really, when all is said and done, simply a high degree of pleasure? A down-to-earth salesman from New York recently raised this point. Rather rudely I answered, "No, pleasure and joy are altogether different things." Smiling, he remarked that he thought he had come to Greece on a pleasure trip. "No doubt!" I replied. It was an awkward moment; he happened to be our guest. How swiftly these misunderstandings arise! "Look," he began, patient already: "Einstein tells us everything's relative. There are no absolutes any more. So we must learn to get along with relative degrees of pleasure and pain as well. Let's leave such high-flown concepts as 'joy' to the poets. Poetry is systematic ambiguity anyhow, and I'll stick to science."

I had to thank our guest for reminding me of certain common illusions—his own, naturally. Einstein of course was all for "absolutes," or rather for provable "constants" like the speed of light. Yet many laymen make him the unwilling apostle of a creed which Saroyan defined as, "No foundation. All the way down the line." Practically everybody nowadays invokes the sanction of science for what he himself believes, or disbelieves. In classical times the Greeks used to invoke the gods like that. The popular consensus has always included some toplofty, cloud-mantled terrain. Once upon a time the gods lived there; now science does. The most valuable Greek thinkers were those who dared question the public image of the gods. It is time to question the mythologema of science likewise.

Theoretical science, in its farthest reaches, is refined rationalism: a kind of intellectual rocketry. It involves kicking free of the body of one's own emotional experience, at a certain stage, in order to push some small payload of comparatively objective thought into orbit. Ideas are more important, in scientific work, than emotion. But scientists themselves do not pretend that thoughts are therefore truer than feelings—or that feelings are mere matters of degree. This poisonous public fallacy arises from a superstitious reading of scientific method.

Yet why shouldn't science, proceeding step by step, eventually build up an accurate, all-inclusive picture of the world? An objective picture at last! The basic method, of course, would be scientific observation of cause and effect in nature. But this goes just a little way. Beyond our limited ken such observation is impossible. And the plain fact is that there are no plain facts. All nature, all of it, stands rooted in the unobservable. Think of procreation, for instance, or space time, or quantum mechanics, or electromagnetism, or, for that matter, thought. We cannot observe any of these basic realities. We see some of their manifestations, and that's all. So we spin theories to account for them. Then we look for data to accommodate our theories. Such data we may indeed find. But meanwhile a most comforting assurance has been lost to us. Insensibly, somewhere along the line, *seeing is believing* has become its own opposite: *believing is seeing*. At this point science stands nonplussed before the gates of paradox. Objectively (which is to say *as* science in the accepted sense) it cannot pass the gates.

Astrophysics offers a rather dramatic case in point. At the moment the chief astronomical observatories rock and groan with debate over this fundamental question: is the universe expanding, just possibly contracting, or holding steady by dint of continuous creation? No agreement on the matter seems in sight. Each authority's answer depends upon his choice of data and of algebra, and finally upon his temperament. For example a leading "steady state" theorist upholds his own view as being the most "esthetically satisfying." To himself, naturally. We are back in the realm of the subjective. Astrophysics calls old-time metaphysics irresistibly to mind. Just imagine three preachers plunging into this debate. A proponent of the "expanding" theory might well thunder: *In the beginning was the Word* (John 1:1). His colleague on the side of "contracting" could retort: *And the heavens departed, as a scroll is rolled up* (Rev. 4:14). Finally the "steady state" minister would rise: *And God said unto Moses, I AM THAT I AM* (Exod. 3:14). Sir Arthur Eddington, himself an "expanding" man, put the matter in a nutshell: "There are no purely observational facts about the heavenly bodies . . . The so-called facts are in any case theoretical interpretations." Narrow in all the way from the cosmos to the atom, and that statement still holds good.

Microcosmic theory, perhaps more advanced, even includes a basic "uncertainty principle." Some Oriental thinkers smilingly welcome "uncertainty" as a return to ancient Chinese notions of Fate as a Dice-Player. It does shake up determinism. The very dots on the dice keep switching as they roll! Or, to substitute a still more appropriate game, there is just no way of labeling the infinitesimal billiard balls upon a microcosmic pool table. In tracing the movement of a particular ball we lose its position relative to the others. Conversely, in pinpointing its position at one moment we fail to follow its roll. But on the other hand all this does not imply that microcosmic events are uncertain in themselves. It is just that we can never be precise about them. Microphysics remains a highly conjectural and even rather subjective study. Louis de Broglie, a subatomic billiards ace, uncompromisingly states the position: "It has been said of art that it was 'Man added to Nature.' The same definition also applies to science."

This intrusion of the subjective aspect makes science more difficult but also more rewarding than ever, for specialists and amateurs alike. Theoretical science fairly hums, nowadays, with mysteries which echo each man's nearest and dearest mystery: himself. Meanwhile it seems steadily less likely that scientific engineers in radiation-resistant smocks will ever put the universe in man's pocket. We really have no right to dream of an objective world-picture. Instead, scientific progress on a technical level may actually destroy all the evidence—like tossing an unsolved problem into the fire.

Getting back to joy: what distinguishes joy from pleasure is not that joy is "bigger" in itself but that it has to do with a larger order of experience than pleasure does. Wordsworth found in the rainbow a shining example of that larger order:

> *My heart leaps up when I behold*
> *   A rainbow in the sky:*
> *So was it when my life began;*
> *So is it now I am a man;*
> *So be it when I shall grow old,*
> *   Or let me die!*

Such a sentiment, if applied to merely pleasure-giving objects (a dry martini, a Mercedes-Benz, a hi-fi set, a ham sandwich) would be manifestly absurd. Incidentally, is there any "systematic ambiguity" in Wordsworth's lines? The greatest poetry, it seems to me, is always spontaneous and invariably precise. It occurs where the meaning and the music merge; it stands clear as mathematical equations; or it flutters like brave and vivid pennants in the sun, over the battlements of prose. The Hellenistic poet Menander said much the same thing as Wordsworth, but in less militant and more magnificent style. Gilbert Murray's translation well preserves the clean, sweeping winds of the original:

> *I count it happiness,*
> *Ere we go quickly thither whence we came,*
> *To gaze ungrieving on these majesties:*
> *The world-wide sun, the stars, water and clouds,*
> *And fire. Live Pármeno, a hundred years*
> *Or a few months, these you will always see,*
> *And never, never, any greater things.*

The American poet Robert Lax conjures up the same truth in a lighthearted juggling act which uses winged words instead of hoops or sparklers.

> *live always*
> *(my friend)*
> *as if you*
> *had world*
> *as if you*
> *had world*
> *as if you*
> *had world . . .*
>
> *live always*
> *(my friend)*
> *as if you*
> *had world*
> *as if you*
> *had world*
> *enough*
> *and time.*

It is worth noting that the shadow of death, however subtly, forms one single background for all three of these widely separated hymns to joy. In the same way, the much-discussed "tragic sense" of ancient Greece served as a sort of dark landscape for the flowering of classical culture—the most joyous culture, perhaps, that the world has yet known. Life to the Greeks was an adventure: beautiful, fine, far-ranging, fearful too, and of course fatal at the last.

This brings me to the second distinguishing characteristic of joy, which is release: a momentary rising on the wings of the dawn, beyond the reach of Fate's ready hammer, even if only for an instant—flung high like the little singing lark on a spring morning, singing and winging clear into the gold. Joy at its uttermost is ecstasy. (In the original Greek, "ecstasy" meant literally "standing outside" of oneself.) Nothing but ecstasy can break your bonds and seize you so out of your accustomed self that you cease to know yourself as mortal flesh or even as a "self" at all. You become instead the lark which "at heaven's gate sings."

Sophocles put the matter with his usual calm perfection when he said, "The joy that surprises and transcends our hopes is like in fullness to no other." Yet we remain caged birds, by and large. Or our wings are clipped. Earth-bound, we dread the tawny tabby on the wall. Instead of singing, we scratch in the dirt and scold. How came this to be? How have we lost our lightheartedness, which was our freedom? Was it by eating of the fruit of the tree of knowledge? Maybe so. Why not? I find it easier to believe in that sort of "original sin" than to believe every American bombed Hiroshima. If it is true that "no man is an island," neither is every man a murderer. Most of our "guilt feelings" are like suitcases stuffed with bad news—burdensome, yet easy enough to carry. They provide handy excuses, too, for our so seldom attempting to sing or to soar.

Curiously, all of us have met people, here and there, who really are happy a large part of the time. They themselves know full well that they are happy, right down to their fingertips, and they show it. (Our vegetable-man is one such.) As with their joy, so with their suffering; it also can be very great. Yet they go on saying "Yes" to life. For though all of us without exception face death at last, not all of us are sick all the time. The world is not a sanatorium, it is a heaven defiled.

The Bull Mountain was once covered by lovely trees. But it is near the capital of a great state. People came with their axes and choppers; they cut the woods down, and the mountain lost its beauty. Yet even so the day air and the night air came to it, rain and dew moistened it. Here and there fresh sprouts began to grow. But soon cattle and sheep came along and browsed on them and in the end the mountain became bare and gaunt, as it is now . . . To us too, as to the mountain, comes the air of day, the air of night. Just at dawn, indeed, we have for a moment and in a certain degree a mood in which our promptings and aversions come near to being such as are proper to man. But something is sure to happen before the morning is over . . .

Those gloomy words, translated by Arthur Waley, might have been written last week. But in fact they come from a Chinese philosopher named Mencius, twenty-four centuries back. Mencius believed that long before his own day dawned, there had been a golden age. Like the ancient sages of every race he assumed that once upon a time—as naturally as a mountain bears forests—mankind rejoiced. It may well be true. Nostalgia for a lost paradise will not help us, however. If we must feel nostalgic, let it be for No Nostalgia, and for faith in better dawnings to come. Lord Dunsany has a story in which the wildflowers complain to Great God Pan. Their meadows are being paved and cindered over, gradually destroyed by man. "Be patient, my friends," Pan tells them, "for just a little longer." To me the dreams of childhood and youth seem just such wildflowers. We murder them; yes, those we do murder! They pass; yet in each new generation they endure. And they endure in art.

Suppose we had been sitting close under the organ of a great cathedral at High Mass. The music seemed to reconstruct the very stones. Song and incense cloud and arch and column all became the same, like one fountain. But now the organ tones fold flashing into silence, nothingness. Or perhaps we were strolling about the Breughel Room at Vienna when suddenly the walls opened inward. It was an interior awakening to a single vivid image of the whole world. Each separate picture seemed a facet of the same radiance. What did it illuminate? We cannot remem-

ber. The colors shift and fade like fireworks falling away. Or say
we took our ease within an open-sky architecture such as the
Temple of the Sun in Mexico, the Tom Quad at Oxford, the
Piazza San Marco at Venice or the fiery, cliff-backed phoenix
which is Delphi. Remembering the weightless splendor, what
survives? Only the quickening of dream.

> *O let me never with folly live,*
> *But still be found where the garlands are:*
> *For you know the singer, old as he is,*
> *Sings of remembrance even now:*
> *And still of Heracles . . .*

It was on the wild island of Salamis, in a book-lined sea cave, that
old Euripides wrote those lines. Euripides sings of remembrance
even now. After twenty-four centuries, he still is found where
the garlands are. Therefore they say that life is brief and art is
long. But not so for us. Because whatever art may build it must always build anew, within the majesties of passing life, and within
the stormy blue abyss and forest of the human heart. Where October reigns all year round and the red and yellow leaves fall
thick as stars across the darkening glade, art is brief indeed—and
life is long. Yes, life is long and long for the shivering huntsman;
he will have time for many a vision art bestows. Many a time will
art give him a glimpse of his quarry racing afar, like a dappled
doe glimpsed in the distance through the falling leaves. He spurs
on after it, into the night.

Art often revolves about the fact of death. It turns on man's
eternal effort to reconcile life's welcome with the end of life.
Consider the north-European epics for example: *Burnt Njal,*
Grettir the Strong, Tristan, The Song of Roland, Le Morte
d'Arthur, Siegfried, Beowulf. Some might say that "Gothic
gloom" accounts for their prevailing unity. If so, what about the
Iliad? In fact the earliest of all surviving epics, composed some

two thousand years before Homer, is also a meditation upon death. Towards its climax the Sumerian hero, Gilgamesh, sets out on a final adventure. He knows neither what nor where it will be. Hear the lament (from N. K. Sandars' brilliant translation) with which Gilgamesh goes to meet his fate:

> *Why should I not wander over the pastures in search of the wind? My friend, my younger brother . . . who was very dear to me and who endured dangers beside me, Enkidu, my brother, whom I loved, the end of mortality has overtaken him. I wept for him seven days and nights till the worm fastened on him. Because of my brother I stray through the wilderness and cannot rest . . . How can I be silent, how can I rest, when Enkidu whom I love is dust, and I too shall die, and be laid in the earth forever?*

Deliberately, as if to force himself onto a new plain of courage, Gilgamesh goes to sleep where lions roam. The moon rises. He awakens to find the great beasts all about him, "glorying in life." He journeys on, to the gates of a mountain which guards the setting sun. The dragon-tailed guardians, whose very look is death, greet Gilgamesh sympathetically. He enters the mountain and marches in utter darkness for twelve leagues. At last he comes out to the sparkling playground of the gods. There Shamash, the sun-god, accosts him. The god is saddened, fatherly: "Gilgamesh, you will never find the life for which you are seeking." But the hero replies: "Now that I have toiled and strayed so far over the wilderness, am I to sleep and let the earth cover my head for ever? Let my eyes see the sun until they are dazzled with looking. Although I am no better than a dead man, still let me see the light of the sun!" Then the "Lady of the Vine" intercepts him briefly:

> *"Gilgamesh, where are you hurrying to? You will never find the life for which you are looking. When the gods cre-*

ated man they allotted to him death, but life they retained in their own keeping. As for you, Gilgamesh, fill your belly with good things; day and night, night and day, dance and be merry, feast and rejoice. Let your clothes be fresh, bathe yourself in water, cherish the little child that holds your hand, and make your wife happy in your embrace; for this too is the lot of man."

Gilgamesh will not listen; he goes on. He locates a shadowy ferryman and a mystic boat with idols for ballast. He smashes the idols. He makes a sail out of the skins he has been wearing. Naked, he steps aboard. He stands firmly amidships, himself a mast, clutching his sail of skins. Illimitable winds hurry him across illimitable seas. He reaches an island of bliss. One old couple only abides there, forever exempted from death. It is a very ancient savior of the race, Utnapishtim by name, and his bride. Utnapishtim sprawls at ease in a bower. He lifts his head to look at Gilgamesh. He opens his mouth and speaks:

"As for you, Gilgamesh, who will assemble the gods for your sake, so that you may find the life for which you are searching? But if you wish, come and put it to the test: only prevail against sleep for six days and seven nights." But while Gilgamesh sat there resting on his haunches, a mist of sleep like soft wool teased from the fleece drifted over him, and Utnapishtim said to his wife, "Look at him now, the strong man who would have everlasting life, even now the mists of sleep are drifting over him." His wife replied, "Touch the man to wake him, so that he may return to his own land in peace, going back through the gate by which he came."

Gilgamesh is old now, and worn out. But there is a flower which can restore his lost youth. As a parting gift, Utnapishtim tells him where to find the flower. And he does, but he does not gulp it down. Why not? Has something happened inside Gilga-mesh? Maybe the welcome he found everywhere is working in him now, to round him home again:

"Come here and see this marvelous plant . . . I will take it to Uruk of the strong walls; there I will give it to the old men to eat. Its name shall be 'The Old Men Are Young Again'; and at last I shall eat it myself and have back all my lost youth."

The journey home is long. Midway, a serpent snatches and swallows the magic flower. Just like that. It sloughs its skin and glides away, renewed.

Is this a sad story? I call it comforting. An affirmation of wel-come waiting in the very gates of death. What if the gates them-selves be unalterable?

Or am I somehow morbid about this? Not long ago I got fair warning from a brilliant satirist. "Don't throw the ashes of age and death around," he protested. "Death can drop dead!" And he went on to suggest that the magic flower which Gilgamesh lost to the serpent may actually grow again. Men have longed for it all down the centuries, no doubt of that. Now science may find it at last. The magic flower, mass-produced this time: a pill which can prolong a person's life indefinitely.

It has been urged that the great nations put their shoulders to this task: manufacturing a flower of eternal youth. It could be a crash program, bigger than the building of the Bomb, bigger than the space race, and even more fateful for mankind. Worse, too, I think. It would mean denying all future generations, canceling them right out of our limited living room. No more kids; just us; proud squatting flesh.

Methus'lah lived nine hunderd years!
Methus'lah lived nine hunderd years!
But who calls dat livin'

When no gal'll give in
To no man what's NINE hunderd years?

Say the girl was the same age. Isn't there a certain weariness about the scene? Regardless of their physical condition. Such self-perpetuating folk would be a burden on the earth, a stye in the eye of space time. How could they love? I would rather take poison than a "Methuselah Pill." My reason being, paradoxically enough, that I love this life so much. Simply to breathe is sweet; to see the sun is glorious; to make love is paradise. But a part of the bliss, the glory and the sweetness is inborn, after all. It is each man's spiritual capital: his sense of welcome. Surely to outstay one's own sense of welcome on earth would be dangerous? With insanity the likeliest result?

Already our own land is old, old, and our people the oldest race of all. Let those who say our culture is not joyous note that, too. Joy comes hardest to the very old, and when it breaks upon them at last it may be as a storm, an unsupportable storm, bringing death. Sophocles says, and he means it: "Throughout the future, near and far, as throughout the past, shall this law hold good: Nothing that is vast enters into the life of mortals without a curse." Yet here I am not Sophocles' man. For I say: let the curse come then, if vast joy requires it. We must either learn to bear the storms of joy or else die unmourned and for nought.

What is it that makes our fair land so old, so sad, so desperate? How came we to build this coast-to-coast barbecue pit? I do not know, nor do I care to dwell on the subject. It is true, I suppose, that we have been the first inventors and consumers of most mass manufactures—or, in other words, of what goes to make life "modern." So we are old to the round world, just as Egypt for example was old to the Mediterranean world of four thousand years ago. Indeed, we have a great deal in common with the ancient Egyptians. They suffered a scientific priesthood wherein resided most of the country's higher learning and real power. We have a priestly sciencehood; it is the same thing. Also they were "materialists" like us and "cheerful" like us. And constantly at war with an imitative, swelling Eurasian force, again like us. (Both sides practiced "total warfare" in those days too, by the way: they sowed salt in defeated cities so that not even grass could grow amongst the ruins.) Finally, the ancient Egyptians were wont to deny death, as we are. Their vaunted cheerfulness lay in such denial, for they took the useless relics of earthly life with them into the darkness of the tomb—as into a bomb shelter or a basement rumpus room.

We Americans often try to deny death by denying immortality. For, if the dead are nothing, death itself is nothing either. Or it shrinks at least to the proportions of a macabre joke. Such is the true story of Charles Willson Peale's last words. As he lay dying, Peale breathed to the daughter at his bedside: "Sybilla, feel my pulse." She told him she could feel none. "I thought not," Peale murmured equably, and that was all. Then there is the brisk vignette in an early Marx Brothers film—Groucho bending down to test the pulse of some traffic-victim, and announcing: "Either this man is dead, or my watch has stopped!" Yet what makes that a great comic moment is the element of mystery it still contains: Groucho, with lifted eyebrows and cigar, confronting the Inscrutable. We are not, after all, quite so cavalier about death as we may seem.

When Beowulf died, his people laid the Saxon hero in a longship by the shore. They put his weapons near to hand. They gave him a coverlet of precious stones. They nailed his golden banner to the mast. Then they let the tide take the vessel away. "And no one, whether warrior or wise man, can say who received that cargo." But no easy journey was implied. The mingled rage of Earth, Air, Fire and Water were all to be surmounted and forgot as the hero plunged and lifted, dolphin-like, within the tidal wave of eternity. Could a merely "unexceptionable" soul ride out that wave and sail on, through storms of joy, to joy itself? Does heaven await the good, or the heroic? Or are its requirements harder still? Who will be an unlost voyager?

That question naturally gives rise to another: is there a heaven outside the little that we know of space time? And this must remain open for some of us. We simply have no evidence to go on—either one way or the other—beyond the scriptures and the firm beliefs of men. But we do know about heaven-on-earth: a heaven rooted in the physical and yet not physical. This heaven, when you find it, is a lucky landfall and a temporary ease. It is an ephemeral island of bliss, storm-ringed, so hard to discover, and hell to leave again. Yet again it awaits you. The timid folk who say this heaven is no more than a dream, lie. For here the evidence is overwhelming. Art, music and literature abound with goods from this island. Only geography is ignorant of heaven-on-earth, and the storms of joy obscure it. But many, many sailors-in-the-spirit (including your neighbor, perhaps, or your child, or yourself?) have been there and come back again. Such tempestuous, dangerous and glorious voyages, it seems to me, are the best possible preparation for the last one of all—wherever that may lead.

If you cannot trim your ship through storms of joy, have you even the right to hope for heaven? Yet we are taught to handle mooring lines, not sails. "Pray it out" and "Talk it out" are the characteristic portside instructions. The assumption being that our illicit yearnings would swamp us if we failed to air them, one way or the other. True, a majority of our yearnings appear to be either illicit or else downright silly, which is worse. But what about our sense of adventure and our capacities for tackling the storms of joy? Here the solemn guardians of our souls and minds throw up their hands, so often, in pale consternation: "No, no!" they cry. "Such storms could really rock the boat. Best hide from them!" The alternative however is just rotting in harbor—so long as the harbor remains, or the illusion of it remains, to shelter us. Meanwhile we know the pleasures and repressions of the waterfront. These are not joy.

Have you built your ship of death, O have you?
O build your ship of death, for you will need it.

Such has been the cry of seers, philosophers and prophets from the beginning. There must be something in it. But the words given here come from a recent and maligned prophet indeed. D. H. Lawrence wrote them shortly before his own death in 1930. Three years before that, he showed the more acid side of his thinking in a letter to a psychoanalyst: "You can convince a man that he lusts after his grandmother—he doesn't mind!—but how are you going to bring him to see that as an individual he's a blown egg?"

The chiefest and best root of joy is yet to be described. Yet it cannot be. For this is something numb in itself, gnarled, dark in dark. One puny word, *instinct*, must stand for this life line into the earth.

Joy springs from the free play of our deepest instincts. But aren't instincts apt to be criminal? Not so! That gloomy doctrine is only a perversion of Freud's teaching that criminal desires are generally repressed. "Repressed" and "profound" are two different things. Deepest in the heart of man lies good, not evil. As a means of showing this let me return once more to Sophocles' *Antigone*. Here is the story: A certain enemy of Thebes has fallen in battle and the Theban king decrees that he must lie unburied—a feast for dogs and ravens. But Antigone, the dead man's sister, disobeys the command; she gives her brother an honorable burial. As punishment, the king buries Antigone herself alive. So much for the tragedy, which like all the Greek tragedies was intended to raise some basic questions about human behavior. For instance, was it the king or Antigone who obeyed instinct? And which was really the criminal? The answers must be obvious. The Bible very often raises similar questions. For example, when Herod ordered the Massacre of the Innocents, did he trust his deepest instincts, or was it the dictates of policy? Again, which did the Good Samaritan follow? Show me the man who, upon re-flection, still maintains that the deepest human instincts are crimi-nal—and I'll show you one of the solemn and frowning sort for whom life is not life but a disaster!

We may yet prove worthy of heaven, providing that we ac-cept the great truths of life on earth. What truths? What are the fundamentals of this present existence? The highly proper poet, T. S. Eliot, lists three: "birth, copulation and death"—which only goes to show where propriety will get you. That reduction may spell the survival of the race, but not individual fulfillment. In-stead, I make it: birth, joy and death. Each of these three goes beyond the physical to touch eternity. They are the good storms that change everything here. To experience them is to have lived.

Imagine for a moment that we are sailing the blue waters of the Aegean Sea, out past Cape Sounion. There are dolphin hereabout, and our presence amuses them. So they come swiftly slipping through their watery underworld to the side of our boat. And now each smooth separate dolphin makes his leap, by us, by us; he rises into the sparkling air and goes under again; from blue up into gold and down again, almost a sunshine-woven shadow as he shudders down the darkness and returns, and leaps again: the glisten, jet and joy of him arching, arching—footless fellow slip-pery upon the footless air. The joy of it!

Thus a life should be: one sudden sliding gliding leap into space, time and air, breathing deep like the dolphin at the top of his arc, then smoothly down-turning, welcoming the depths, and so gone once more.

Had we sufficient sense of joy, each of our lives in its entirety might be like that.

THE EARTHBORN ART

Men used to pour lightnings of the spirit into cold forms. They gave radiance to stillness. They made marble ripple and swell. They caused bronze to breathe before the bewildered eye. The ancient Greeks could shape "dead" matter to outrival life itself. No other statuary compares with theirs. What was their secret strength? It rested mainly, I believe, in a clear understanding that sculpture is the earthborn art. Painting and architecture also relate to the earth, but painting mainly conveys a sense of atmosphere, while architecture primarily shapes interior space. Only sculpture keeps its earthly origins intact and

45

gives first of all the feeling "here I stand." In fact it was first designed to stand on holy ground.

The earliest Greek worship centered on groves or springs. One tree would be singled out for particular veneration: often a tree struck by lightning, touched by the dread weapon of Father Zeus. When the tree fell, the stump remained sacred. To show this, it would be carved: rough-hewn into an image of the god himself. In the course of time, sheds were built to protect these warning figures. From this grew, by slow stages, the great temples and divine images of the classical period. The statues never degenerated into idols until Hellenistic times. Their purpose was to show the sanctity of the place where they stood. As if to say: "The god represented here feels at home here."

The Greeks had a saying of great simplicity and weight which was: "Begin at the hearth." Every Greek infant who survived his first five days upon earth was carried around the family hearth by way of celebration, and acceptance. Holy places too were hearths. There gods and men gathered. And since the gods came to have statues at such places, their worshipers followed suit. To show the difference between mortal and divine, the so-called "votive" statues were kept relatively small. They stood adoring, with arms outstretched, like little listeners for the heartbeat of the world. The most astonishing treasure of votive figurines yet unearthed is to be seen in the National Museum of Cyprus. Most of them are human, yet daimons and half-animal totems also take part. They are two thousand all told, grouped in a semicircle, worshiping together. Twenty-seven centuries back they stood just so about a hearthstone of Earth herself.

From Odysseus to Yuri Gagarin, far-voyagers instinctively have kissed the earth upon returning home. This would seem an ideal ending for the journey of life as well. And therefore the last resting place of the heroic dead is "consecrated ground." It always has been. So a statue at the tomb of a Greek hero was there to show that a great soul sanctified the place.

The Greek sculptures of athletes began as votive figures of still another kind, set up in the sacred precincts of the Pan-Hellenic Games. The Games themselves were holy, held in honor of particular gods: Zeus at Olympia and Nemea, Poseidon at Corinth and Apollo at Delphi. In each case the most demanding contest was the five-ply pentathlon which included wrestling, discus, javelin, broad-jump and sprint. A pentathlon winner, it was said, had the right to erect a votive statue. Until the days of their decline the Greeks believed that only an all-round athlete could be truly godlike. Their statues of athletes were meant to honor not men alone, but gods. In fact art and athletics were but two sides of a single radiance, the sunshine of the Greek soul: *areté*. The word translates as *excellence* but it implied a great deal more than being first and best. *Areté*, in any endeavor, carried with it the unmistakable bloom of perfection. It meant "firmly seizing the beautiful," as Aristotle said. It fulfilled what is swift, powerful, passionate, shining with the light of eternal grace. Godlikeness was the athlete's real aim, and victory his proof.

> *Single is the race, single*
> *Of men and of gods;*
> *From a single mother we both draw breath.*
> *But a difference of power in everything*
> *Keeps us apart . . .*
> *Yet we can in greatness of mind*
> *Or of body be like the immortals,*
> *Though we know not to what goal . . .*
> *Fate has written that we shall run.*

Those lines from the Olympic poet Pindar give the crux of the matter. The key to the ancient Greeks is *areté:* they strove to act like gods. And the key to Greek sculpture also is *areté:* earthborn grace and force so shaped as to enhance a sacred place.

Appropriately enough, the first full-scale Greek sculptures

may represent either men or gods. Nobody knows which, and so they are called simply "Kouros" ("Youth") carvings. The best of these, dating from the seventh century B.C., was found on the Aegean island of Melos. The bare marble in the Athens Museum gives a pawky notion of the vanished reality. Originally the figure stood outdoors, in the dappled light of a sacred grove. In those days its flesh, hair and features were stained with brilliant colors. The statue seemed to walk there on the island, a real youth. And if its debt to ancient Egyptian models is apparent, so are three great innovations. In Egypt only slaves went naked. By contrast this aristocratic figure is entirely nude. Secondly the storied "archaic smile" illuminates the statue, as if it were bringing good news from the happy gods. Finally the Egyptian canon of human proportions has been thrown right overboard to produce a younger, stronger, springier, deeper-breathing, more athletic ideal. It makes one think of Pindar's prayer for foot-racers: "Grant them with feet so light to pass through life!"

Sculptors of the next century, the sixth, excelled at bas-relief. Prize examples at Athens, adorning the pedestals of statues long-since lost, show a rugby-like scrimmage with a small ball, wrestling, and something the books call "hockey" although it was probably a kind of lacrosse. The illusion of deep space was lacking from these bas-reliefs: action took place laterally on a narrow stage. The limitation made for artistic unity on the whole, but problems of perspective did arise. For instance it appears that the man who carved the "Wrestlers" meant to place a broad-jumper and a linesman on a plane behind theirs. But the effect he got resembles a zoomar lens photo, with the background figures crowded up against the contestants. Indeed, the art of all such bas-reliefs mingles poetry and prose: precise conventions clashing with exact descriptions. Not until the succeeding century, the golden age of Greek sculpture, did the two merge perfectly.

The "Charioteer" is almost all that remains of a life-size bronze that once included the chariot and four horses besides. In ancient times, as now, the men who raced fast horses were less honored than the men who owned them: racing has always been the sport of kings, or millionaires, and it was one such victor who commissioned this thank-offering to Apollo. He laid it up in the treasury of the god at Delphi, where it remains today. The figure is complete except for one arm. The remaining hand still clutches the reins of the horses—which must have been wrenched free by some fur-clad marauder. The horses and chariot, doubtless, were melted down in a dark age to make armor, bullets or pots. By some miracle the figure, a revelation in itself, was spared. Stillness is the statue's chief quality, stillness elevated to an essential virtue. The charioteer moves no more than need be, yet the still grace of his stance sufficiently hints at all that he might do with four mettlesome horses in the dust and clangor of a crowded turn. In poise he resembles a high-diver or a fencing master or an acrobat, or a young tree in the wind that keeps raising its green crest straight up again.

There are two clues as to how this extraordinary grace was achieved, one technical and the other philosophical. First the technical point: it is now realized that the model for the "Charioteer" must have been carved in wood. A clay mold was made from the model, and the solid bronze cast therein. Afterwards the bronze was elaborately chased. The youth's diadem was damascened with silver; he received separate bronze eyelashes and onyx eyes with enameled whites; his lips were inlaid with red copper. Yet all this fine work served only to enhance the still finer simplicity of the artist's conception, which sprang straight from his sensitive use of wood. The "Charioteer" stands like a young tree because he came from one!

The second clue rests in the old philosophic problem of the One and the Many. Archaic sculptors strove to produce and reproduce one ideal type. There were distinct formulas for carving the ears, eyes, nose, mouth, hair, hands, drapery—everything in fact. This made for strong, arbitrary patterns, as in formal poetry.

It meant constant reiteration of single archetypal forms underlying nature's infinite variety. Archaic sculptors grasped the
principle of the One but not of the Many; they ignored the little
differences that make each person unique; they showed ideal
man in various poses but never individual men. Then along came
the creator of the "Charioteer," early in the fifth century B.C.,
and took both these principles in his hands together. This marked
the transition from archaic to classical Greek sculpture. The
artist retained the traditional, semiabstract patterning of hair,
face and tunic; he composed the entire figure out of practically
mathematical exactitudes. Yet on the other hand he changed
everything—from the tilt of the head to the thrust of the toes—a
trifle, just enough to shake the formal fabric with the breath of
life. What might have seemed cut and dried, however beautiful,
he made real and warm. What might have been merely an ideal
athlete now became a unique individual.

The Ancients believed that their gods existed in the physical
and not merely symbolic sense. This might of imagination, giving
solid form to quicksilver concepts, was a primal source of the
Greek genius at its height. Imagination in this full sense of the
word has left us, by and large. We hear breakers resounding in a
sea-cave; but the Ancients heard old Triton also trumpeting
there. We see white caps; they saw nereids. We may wistfully
acknowledge a poetic metaphor; they felt the presence of the
gods. There lies the heart of the matter: it makes all the difference between Homer and, say, Tennyson. Or between Paul Man-
ship's "Prometheus" at Rockefeller Center and the fifth-century
"Zeus" at Athens—the greatest sculpture we possess.

This life-size bronze was found in the sea off Artemision. The
circumstance may have helped to persuade people, by an unconscious process of analogy, that it represents Poseidon, Earth-
Shaker, god of the wine-dark sea. The statue is generally labelled
"Poseidon," and the guides will tell you that it once held a trident

ready to hurl like a javelin. But the trident, Poseidon's invariable attribute, was a classical equivalent of the modern tunny fork, or fisherman's spear; it was meant for thrusting, not for throwing. The traditional thunderbolt of cloud-gathering Zeus fits the position much better. Furthermore the same Athens museum contains a statuette of Zeus that must have been modeled on this masterpiece, still brandishing the thunderbolt.

Ancient doctors maintained that the best years for begetting children lay between the ages of thirty and fifty-five, the prime of life for active men. Presumably Zeus falls within those age limits, since he was both Father of the Gods and immortal. His striding form is electric with young, self-renewing energy. His image seems no more "sexual" than that of a lion or a fighting bull, yet it does radiate virility. Also it looks impassive and implacable, swift as an eagle, firm as an oak, fine-drawn as a spider's web, smooth as a wave, tall as a hill . . . The statue was intended not only as an object of worship but also as an inspiration to men. Remove the imagined thunderbolt, picture a javelin balanced there instead, and one sees a mortal warrior or an athlete in the games. The god resembles a man, who resembles a god. Here dissolves the "difference of power in everything" that separates men from the gods. This manifests precisely what Pindar proclaimed:

> *Yet we can in greatness of mind*
> *Or of body be like the immortals.*

War between Athens and Sparta brought the brilliant fifth century to a ruinous close. Men no longer kept faith with the gods. Philosophy and science soared, since the owl of Athena, wisdom's bird, "flies only with the coming of dusk." But in that same moment the muses dance off to bed. The arts all declined, though slowly. Sculpture now became more subtle in concept and supple in shape than ever before or since, yet its spirit was less. A prize example of such work is the heroic "Ballplayer" at the Athens museum. This was modeled in wet clay rather than wood. After the clay had hardened it was given a skin of hot wax, into which the artist fingered and incised the final details. Then the sculpture was encased in a clay mold with tubes inserted here and there. Over a very hot fire the wax melted and ran out, to be replaced with molten bronze. Once the bronze had hardened the inner clay core was chipped out. Finally the hollow bronze was closed up, burnished and perfected at every point. This "lost wax" method of casting gave heady, dangerous freedom to the sculptor. It freed him first from the labor and discipline of actual carving, second from the constraint of balancing heavy masses solidly.

When Homer's hardiest heroes are wounded or slain he will suddenly refer, for pathos, to their "tender flesh." Fourth-century sculptures, having been modeled in soft clay, could well express this sort of tenderness. And being light they could twist and cantilever out from their pedestals, gesturing with new grace and ease.

Estheticians, who have so little to talk about, delight in praising the sculptures of this period for what they call "intelligibility of pose." This means you can see what the statue is supposed to be doing. For instance the "Ballplayer" spirals in such a manner as to display the whole motion of his body to viewers in every direction. He may well be fielding a ball. Yet who can say that this is not Paris of Troy, hesitantly and with pounding heart awarding the golden apple to Aphrodite? There is a curious air of gloom about the man, as if he had just doomed Troy—or walked a batter? In Sparta the words "youth" and "ballplayer" were synonymous. And whether or not he really was intended to represent a ballplayer, this bronze youth does have the true ballplayer's capacity for concentration along with a great athlete's build. He looks a bit liverish, though, and not simply because the bronze is liver-colored. Contemporary writings show that athletes of the fourth century tended—as now—to overtrain and become hypochrondriacs. Specialization was beginning to drive them to it. Athletes balanced on a razor's edge of refinement. So did art.

Yet it remained capable of incredible loveliness and depth. Consider for instance "Hermes with the Infant Dionysus" by Praxiteles. This particular work offers a great deal more than meets the eye. Of course Praxiteles' magic name gives the piece unparalleled rarity-value. It is the single surviving major statue attributed directly to a known Greek genius. We have nothing by Pheidias, or Myron, for example. The Parthenon marbles were only supervised by Pheidias, and Myron's "Discus-Thrower" is a reconstruction. As for the "Winged Victory" and "Venus de Milo" at the Louvre, these are great themes from the hands of nameless and comparatively minor Hellenistic sculptors. But the "Hermes" has a clear title dating back to the earliest surviving guidebook. Pausanias—an old Greek sightseer whose travel log is still the archaeologist's bible—describes it and definitely names Praxiteles as the sculptor.

Yet many will testify to being disappointed in the "Hermes" at first. The statue has a room to itself in the little museum at Olympia. It stands perched above a wide surrounding sandbox—put there to break its fall in the unlikely event of earthquake. A red-faced guard with a brigand's mustache sits propped in one corner of the room, nodding, trying to keep awake. He looks so much more human than the statue, and so much better protected. In the center "Hermes" leans, lifting his lost arm, lonely, being stared at. Yet, badly placed, badly lit and broken though he is, "Hermes" still lives. His calm and tender relation to the baby is breathtaking. Meanwhile strangers from a dozen countries pace around the sandbox, pointing and whispering. Then one by one they turn on their heels and walk away. Only a couple of bearded art students linger. To admire the work? No, they are loudly enlarging upon its faults. The statue does have faults, quite a few in fact.

Chances are that Pausanias was only half-right after all. I think

Praxiteles deserves full credit for conceiving the statue but no blame for its execution. The conception is pure genius, while the carving is slick. Moreover, Praxiteles is known to have been a modeler first and foremost, not a stone-carver. Clay was the medium best suited to his subtle, urgent hands. His usual custom therefore was to build up a statue in clay and make a hollow-bronze cast of it. The casting process destroyed the model. So if another client desired the same statue, a marble copy would have to do. Such was often the case. The copies are known to have been carved by Praxiteles' apprentices, under his direction. And internal evidence indicates that the surviving "Hermes" is just such a studio copy from the lost original bronze. The faults that critics find in the statue all appear to stem from its translation into stone.

The modeling, to start with, is too soft and delicate for marble. This always happens when a sculpture that was built up of wet clay gets transferred to the medium of direct stone-carving. It is as if a piece of chamber music were transcribed for trumpets and trombones. But here the balance is off too. The marble figure is half leaning and half pivoting. Hermes looks uncertain where to put his weight. This has been blamed on a restorer who replaced both of his lost shanks and one lost foot besides. It was a difficult assignment, and restorers seldom get things right in any case. But the real difficulty was Praxiteles' own: how to translate a free-standing bronze into a leaning marble figure without drastically altering its position. This translation had to be made because marble is so much heavier than hollow bronze. So Praxiteles introduced the tree stump—a stolid piece of sculpture—for support. Then he added the drapery to hide the conjunction of the stump to the figure. Finally he had to wink at one eyesore: the marble brace connecting the tree with Hermes' hip.

Remove all that and one sees something of the lost original bronze in the mind's eye. I think Hermes held the infant comfortably in the crook of his arm and danced, whirling, sharply pivoting, holding aloft a cluster of dancing grapes to amuse Dionysus. Doubtless the grapes counterbalanced the baby. This enabled Praxiteles to rest his whole bronze on the narrow dancing feet of Hermes alone. The effect must have been gravity-defying, light as a tossed wine cup; a fiery spiral swinging wide at chest-level and then coiling close again to receive the reverse spiral of the dancing grapes. They may well have been separately cast in purplish metal. Possibly Hermes' hair was gilded, but the polished bronze itself would do very well for his sun-browned flesh. For the infant Dionysus, ivory and gold were in order, to make him swing like the dawn in Hermes' arm. There is some evidence for this last guess in the curious crudeness of the marble infant—as if Praxiteles' apprentices had despaired of matching a radiant jewel of a child in cold marble.

Had Praxiteles no pride? What made him agree to produce a marble copy which could never approach the perfection of the bronze? Money and glory, partly. Also, Praxiteles maintained a sizable studio; he was committed to provide work and training for his apprentices. But the main consideration must have been this: he could count on his favorite painter to conceal most of the marble's unavoidable faults and turn it into something alive. This painter, Nikias, was famous in his own right throughout the classical world. He regularly collaborated with Praxiteles on commissions for marble statues, and his were all the final touches. With the "Hermes," Nikias doubtless began by obscuring that awkward tree stump and drapery in unobtrusive shades. The brace he left unpainted so it would blend with the marble niche for the statue. The skin colors he mixed with beeswax, warm, and applied with rags, rubbing and polishing the figures until they fairly sparkled. Little Dionysus would be as white as new-fallen snow, with pink roses in his cheeks, the palms of his outstretched hands and his merrily kicking heels. Hermes' hair was probably sun-yellow, and his body brown like a woodland waterfall, light-filled, all shimmering velocity. Then finally Nikias took up his tiniest brushes to lay in accents of pure color for the lips, nostrils and shining eyes. No longer a statue, here was cold marble at which to warm your hands.

The "Hermes" lost all of Nikias' magic, naturally, in the course of its long sojourn under the earth. We see nothing but the bare stone. Sometimes we even go so far as to declare that bare stone is best, after all. Lacking cake, we prefer dog biscuit. That sort of forced austerity plays its role in modern taste. Worse yet is when our austerity spills over into the realm of ideas. We tend to merely glance at works of art, expecting to be pleased or displeased by their forms, whereas more cultivated generations paid attention to what lay beneath. The realm of ideas is eternal, and in that realm the "Hermes" remains as rich as ever. It happens to spring from the age of Plato and Aristotle. The myths were still revered, but not as matters of fact. Instead, they were taken to be deliberately confusing tales in which ancient wisdom lay concealed. So Praxiteles' task was not merely to illustrate the myth of Hermes and the Infant Dionysus. He went deeper. The "Hermes" is thought made solid, a mine of feeling in unfeeling stone, and the greatest surviving physical document of its time.

The myth from which the statue springs is this: Hermes and Dionysus were half brothers, both fathered by Zeus outside the bonds of marriage. Hera, the awesome wife of Zeus, jealously murdered Dionysus' mother. But Hermes saved the infant by disguising him as a ram and smuggling him off to Mount Helikon, where mountain nymphs would raise him secretly. So what Praxiteles presents is a sort of "Rest on the Flight to Helikon." Here, as in Christian representations of the "Rest on the Flight into Egypt," is shown a peaceful matrix of mighty emotions and huge conflicting forces. The marble moves in the eye of a hurricane. It imparts a sense of delight in danger past, together with the dread of danger still to come. It cradles intimate tenderness in a wide, hostile world, and reveals the seed of the future—glimpsed and gone again—a promise made without speech.

Hermes was a civilizing god. He invented the lyre, the shepherd's pipes, the musical scale, weights and measures, astronomy and the alphabet. The last two make a pair, by the way: Hermes used the constellations as patterns for the first letters. But the fact is that most of his inventions actually hark back to Egypt—where they were credited to Thoth, the ibis-headed god of wisdom. Hermes' alien strain is undeniable, and it usually shows up in his statues. For example, the sculptors who preceded Praxiteles gave Hermes a high pointed helmet, like a sorcerer's cap. The Magi, Persian priests of Zoroaster, wore something similar. (Today it is a dunce cap—strange reversal!) Hermes' helmet was supposed to conceal an inordinately high brow. Often it was winged. We still put feathers in our hats. Some sculptors gave him winged sandals as well, to show that the god was not only quick-thinking but swift as thought besides. Praxiteles, however, scorns all such stage props. On his statue they would be superfluous. Moreover they would act as reminders of Hermes' oriental and mystical side, which the sculptor chooses to ignore. The god he shows is neither a magician nor an intellectual. Secret knowledge is not this Hermes' claim to fame. Nor on the other hand is he a mere messenger-god such as later sculptors portrayed. (Hellenistic, Roman and Renaissance artists were to insult Hermes in their ignorance by giving him a dish-shaped helmet good only in case of rain.) The bareheaded "Hermes" of Praxiteles stands for one thing only, one single virtue which neither rules nor is ruled. I mean intelligence, clear and swift. Praxiteles provides him with a lithe body and a thinking look, and lets him go.

Dionysus also is stripped of religious paraphernalia. Praxiteles even rips away the ram disguise, as previous sculptors never did. Instead of all that, he bodies forth a baby boy delighting in the sunlight on a bunch of grapes. Head and heart are half brothers; together they can work miracles in a dangerous world. The mind conceals and inspires the dark innocent workings of the heart. And so Hermes, pausing in the midst of flight, awakens and entertains his half brother. By the device of the dancing grapes he playfully draws up from Dionysus the beginnings of a force which will one day astonish men and gods alike. The mind awakens the heart's thirst. Hermes is preparing Dionysus, leading his desire towards the great invention that was promised of old.

Soon the boy will bring a new boon to all the world: cooling fire and far music in a garnet chalice, forgetfulness, visions, ecstasy. Dionysus invented wine.

By conquest, Alexander the Great disseminated Greek culture over a vast region, but he spread it thin. The older and more opulent civilizations of the Near East mingled with that of its new rulers; thus Hellenistic art was born. Classical sculpture had recognized four basic subjects: gods, worshipers, heroes and athletes. Hellenistic sculptors of the third and second centuries B.C. multiplied this repertoire and took the world for their province. In the rich cities of the eastern Mediterranean a vast inanimate populace sprang into being. In marble, bronze, porphyry, chalcedony, basalt, ivory, silver, gold and even crystal, they swarmed the parks and porticoes: a motionless host of kings and beggars, gods and geese, children and drunkards, hounds, horses, concubines and fauns. Less than a thousandth part of all this dazzling display remains to us.

It was the time of the first "Statue of Liberty," one hundred and five feet high, bearing a torch, overlooking a harbor and known as the "Colossus of Rhodes." Less famed were the "Aphrodite of Melos" ("Venus de Milo," at the Louvre) and the "Laocoön," a contorted marble nightmare in which serpents slay a prophet and his sons (at the Vatican Museum). All this is vulgar stuff by classical standards, though still zestful and elaborately skilled. By any lesser standards, including those of the Renaissance, it remains marvelous.

The flame of Greek art, flickering lower, yet could work miracles of charm on occasion: witness the Athens "Jockey." Its brilliance is a long way indeed from the anonymous intensity which distinguished the "Kouros" of Melos four centuries back. The difference resembles that between a prayer and a play, so to speak: the "Kouros" is a spirit poised, and the "Jockey" is a personality in action. The latter doubtless was modeled from an actual person. And this merely technical innovation actually marked an important shift in human thought. The growth of empire had brought about a compensating growth of individualism. The old communal ideals, built around the hearth, lay shattered. Now men sought for certainty in themselves and in each other. Art therefore turned personal, various, naturalistic. Chances are that the jockey once had a horse under him, and formed part of a racecourse monument. But tradition hints that he may really have been a "boy on a dolphin." In that case he probably embellished a fountain, perhaps as an outrider for Poseidon, or for foam-born Aphrodite. But he is racing anyway, swift as the wind—his tunic is wonderfully wind-whipped. He bestrides his invisible steed like a very pinwheel of boyish excitement; for him the race is everything. And to look at him brings boyhood back.

There seems never to have been a genuinely "Roman" art, only Greek art commissioned by Romans. Consumer taste prevailed as usual. Hellenistic naturalism slowly gave way to Roman realism: a grim adherence to the physical facts. "Warts and all" sums it up.

About a century before the time of Christ, Apollonius of Athens produced for a Roman client a life-size boxer in bronze, correctly detailed right down to the cauliflower ears, split lips and blood-soaked beard. The statue, now at Rome's Terme Museum, clearly portrayed an actual champion. He was probably a southpaw, since the right side of his head is the worse battered. Otherwise he resembles Rocky Marciano, having the same square-knotted build and rippling back muscles. The Romans, with characteristic lack of poetry, likened such muscles to "mice under the skin." Yet all this uncompromising realism is still a world away from life casts and waxwork dummies. It presents the facts, yes, while arranging them brilliantly and with deceptive casualness. One leg of the statue is four inches shorter than the other for instance, because the proper length would have seemed too long. Not slavish imitation but convincing illusion was the hallmark of Apollonius' art. He was like a conjurer playing with appearances, sure to amaze. Not for him the visions that can change the world; for him the gods remained invisible. The "Boxer" has a melancholy yet indomitable look. One can picture him seated just so in his dressing room after a hard fight, surrounded by reporters. "Well, Champ, how do you feel? What did you use for the knockout? Did the kid hurt you much? Do you look forward to fighting him again?" Aching, wordless, the champion turns and stares.

On such harsh notes Greek art draws towards its close. All things must end, and endings are apt to be harsh. Never again, perhaps, will sculpture succeed in creating men like gods.

Greek sculpture is best seen in relation to the sea-girt land that gave it birth, in brilliant and caressing light. London, Paris, Munich and Rome all have in their museums inspiring glimpses of this art, but once again as in ancient times the best place to get the whole sense of it is on Greek soil. No coldly conscientious eye will do for this experience. The statues hardly need judging, nor are they merely "artistic" triumphs. They have life in them yet, unquenchable. And still they speak, of sacred ground, of men and of the gods. They breathe *areté*. First, last and always are they to be enjoyed, even the gloomy ones. For the joy that springs from utmost endeavor is their one rule.

PROMISED LANDS

IN THE DAYS when the Red Indians possessed most of our continent, a painter named George Catlin went to visit them. No cavalry could follow where he planned to go, and this he knew. But Catlin felt at peace. He just got on his horse, whose name was Charlie, and rode off alone, over the prairie, into the Great West. And into the hearts of men. Sometimes a war party would surround him, all paint and feathers. Grand! Catlin would get out his sketchbook right away. He also sketched the buffalo stampeding like a dusty black flood, and thousands of other things. In all, he visited about fifty savage tribes. How could he communicate? With his eyes, his hands and his pictures. He entered the painted tepees, living for weeks at a time amongst new friends. Many were fierce and proud, some solemn. Others smiled, even laughed at him, and he was loved also. Molested? Never. They made the artist welcome wherever he might wander.

The Indians agreed on what a stranger is. In fact all the most ancient peoples of the world have so agreed. They still do in remote places, and they generally act on this agreement: that a stranger is by definition a pilgrim—"Beloved of God."

We have a different saying now: "The customer is always right." This can turn travel into a kind of daydream. The airline hostess smiles so sweetly; it's her job. Clothes, and money, make the man. Be confident of welcome, or what passes for same. *What can I do for you, please?* See the blind ego ticketed, caressed, stuffed in a bottle and catapulted around the world. Almost at once the projectile is recovered and opened, proving to contain—souvenirs. And what's this, a note? *Help!* it says. Obviously pilgrimage is getting tougher all the time.

Yet the living welcome life, and we welcome each other, and we believe the whole world welcomes us in turn. Such is the sense of welcome; a threefold thing. All of us were blessed with it at birth. However, as everybody knows, the sense of welcome suffers constant attrition from the beginning of school days forward. As one grows, it shrinks. We get to feeling like the fellow in the "Sanforized" ads, half-strangled by his own shirt.

Each person is a part of all the world and yet retains his own steep shores of sense. We are like floating islands, all borne along and nourished by the same life-stream, and yet each one alone, unique. People who deny aloneness do most violence to the sense of welcome. They turn it inside out. The jolly clubman, the cold snob, the ready marcher, the pale churchman, the red-faced child of a Cause—all these are apt to show the sense of welcome reversed. They substitute clannishness, a monkey affair.

Howler monkeys band together ardently. Each crew stakes

out a separate territory in the rain forest. Would-be intruders from other bands get howled down and out in a hurry. Strolling about the Barro Colorado Island in Panama, one constantly crosses the invisible borders of the howlers. Always to torrents of abuse from overhead. "Polite society" is much the same. Try the cocktail circuit in any sizable city, and see.

What people have to say over cocktails is seldom so general, so idealistic and profound as the conversation in a kids' clubhouse. There the talk will pass from sport to sex, to morals, to make-believe, to science, to religion and philosophy with no embarrassment. The sense of welcome binds all these things together for a child, until his elders force him to see them separate. But they do wrong. Specialization should be just a convenience, not a goal. No matter if a man specializes to the point of developing a third eye, he will see no better. Quite the contrary.

Overspecialization makes us less than human. To follow just one way of living and thinking is rather like taking some animal form—permanently. Such ghastly, fairly-tale enchantments were never more common than at present. Most of the adults one meets are sacrifices, so to speak, sacrificed to their own life-programs. So I believe, but many will dispute this. At a cocktail party recently a scientist attempted to set me straight. "Without intense specialization," he began, "we could not develop a sophisticated technology. And without this technology we could not prove scientific advance. For instance we would have no way of understanding the basic constellations in nature—atomic, molecular and cellular. Yet precisely this kind of knowledge is what gives the deepest satisfaction and makes a man intellectually at home. To those of us who really understand it, the world is a crystal palace of space-time structures, mathematically plotted, transparent, and perfectly beautiful!"

Such was the scientist's argument. Twirling his dry martini, did he himself believe it? The point seemed important enough to pursue. Is the scientific vision of the world, to which we have sacrificed so much, really beautiful in itself? I noted aloud that it did not seem to have put much light in the scientist's keen gray eye. At this he blinked, and agreed. "I'm yearning for something more," he explained. "Some further vision. But after physics, what?" The Greek-rooted word for what lies beyond physics is metaphysics, of course. But when I brought *that* up he laughed outright. We looked at each other with a sort of death-grinning despair, and moved apart.

One has reason to suspect a clamminess in joiners, a hollowness in boosters, a veiled threat in fanatics, a grimness about uniforms. Amongst human beings, the pretense of sameness is shameful. Really too high a price to pay for welcome in this world. We want to keep our differences *and* get together. Why not?

Why not?

There was a blind man once who used to walk in the forest, feeling his way from tree to tree in the dark. He was cured of blindness, and afterwards returned to his haunt. "Look," he cried, "the trees are walking!" Absurd, isn't it? Trees don't walk. Or is it that familiarity dulls awareness? Asleep to present mysteries, one feels certain that the woods, at least, never move. Like Macbeth. How can you get together with the man who was blind? The guest becomes a ghost in the house. People seem obvious almost. Or crazy. Perhaps the time has come to change gray thoughts for unknown gold, somewhere far away.

> *I never heard a mocking bird in Kentucky*
> *Spilling its heart in the morning.*
>
> *I never saw the snow on Chimborazo.*
> *It's a high white Mexican hat, I hear.*
>
> *I never had supper with Abe Lincoln.*
> *Nor a dish of soup with Jim Hill.*
>
> *But I've been around.*

With those relaxed lines Carl Sandburg welcomed the world. The more country one actually explores, the better, surely? This remains an open question for some people. A journalist of my acquaintance recently screwed up his courage to ask for a transfer from New York to Europe. "I've been writing foreign news for years now," he explained, "without ever going abroad. I demand to see what I'm discussing!" His editor half rose, transfixing him with a pale burning glance: "Nonsense. All a writer needs is to think, and one can think in a phone booth!"

One can think in a phone booth. One can even telephone. But is a phone booth the place for a full life, or not? The question means something because, as everybody knows, humanity is building itself a warren of phone booths everywhere. My journalist friend would not have found things very different in Europe. They're nailing down the lid all over. Most of us have spent and will spend the greater part of our lives boothed-in. And yet . . .

Remember Courtney and Moe and mighty Tarzan and Eve the tomboy? Remember swaggering Tub with his dog Crack and rough-house Red, and speedy Bones with his kite? Each stands distinct and clear, yet all were as one, for a while. Bones became a priest, I think. Red vanished. Tub sells artificial flavorings and recruits "Fatties Anonymous." Eve works for the League of Women Voters. Tarzan is a cop . . . and so forth. The fuzz has gone off the peach for most of us now. And with it went the sweet, mysterious welcome the world offers first, welcoming us just as we are, which is to say unknown.

Every young child feels the welcome that resides in mystery. Not in one mystery only, but a multitude. Not only in himself but in everyone. All mystery beckons him deeper into life; he enters willingly.

The wide world is a garden to the young in heart. He comes to know danger and charity together, as familiar as light and darkness. Being himself a stranger of the way, an unbidden guest.

With every personal pilgrimage he draws closer to that hidden pilgrim: the ghost, the guest, the secret self within. He comes home shaken and refreshed with mystery. Again he sets forth, hungering still for the immaterial feast of differences: the unfamiliar footfall, the scurrying leaf; the blue gates, the yellow gates and the white gates of dawn.

PART TWO

AIR

Cloud-gathering Zeus, Father of the Gods, in the world's greatest remaining work of sculpture.

At Delphi, the Temple of Apollo, the first European place of pilgrimage, awash with sunlight.

THE REALM
OF THE LIGHTHEARTED

I WAS WALKING in the garden, thinking of Hui-neng, who said: "The marvelous nature of the ordinary person is empty and has no fixed character. One's natural self is a sort of sky." Something made me stop in my tracks. But instead of looking up, I looked down. A fledgling fallen from its nest lay still, stunned and scared at my feet. I picked him up and held him cupped in my hand, to warm the weightless thing. His tiny fluttering heart made my fingers tingle. We gave him something to drink from an eyedropper, and built a little shelter for him in the corner of a wall. There was nothing to do but wait. His parents called en-

71

couragement, they flew down to feed him on occasion, and they too waited.

The chilly, brief spring night came on, and passed. Next day our fledgling seemed stronger. He tried some slight frantic flights. His mother would bustle down and buoy him up for a moment as he floundered. His father swooped to the wall, looked him straight in the eye, and shot up into the trees again like an arrow. They were introducing him to a new dimension. He didn't trust it a bit; hence the wild fluttering. Yet he learned, and by afternoon his new birth had been accomplished: his birth upon empty air. He rose lighthearted to his own domain.

Sometimes he would come back and sing to us. He was braver about people than his brothers were. I felt he did some thinking about us, puzzled though his thought must have been. And I tried to return the compliment by considering, in my equally obscure fashion, his own kind. Birds breathe five times as fast as we do; they live at high-fever temperature; they sing and feast and fly like mad. They keep on interrupting one's daydreams in welcome ways. These air-swimmers can make us feel like bottom-fish. Yet they keep telling us that we too are free—in imagination at least.

If the sky has a world in her keeping, so does imagination. She keeps a hollow round world, light as air, and fully as large as the material one. Art is what stirs this cosmos, making private experience and universal truths interpenetrate. No passports are required. Yet somebody had to discover Troy, and Homer did that. Someone had to go out and listen to Lear outshouting the thunders upon the heath, and Shakespeare did that. The round world of imagination never can be fully explored, let alone conquered. Yet so swiftly does it spin that one may pass almost anywhere within it by remaining still, by hovering a moment.

Some evening in Nicosia, you may happen to stroll through the market district, breathing in rosy dust, harsh cries, stares, sharp colors, hammerings, spices of Araby, charging bicycles. Quick, this way: you duck into a courtyard. No one about. Solitude, suddenly, and silence. The place is an uneven square surrounded by a double tier of archways. Their dark rounded shadows seem more solid than the stone itself. Carved hollows of shadow; quivering columns of light, repeated keyboard-fashion. Now you sense, on the edge of hearing, the cool irregular tune of water dripping into a stone cistern. Architecture, space and the music seem as one.

For centuries this place was known as the "Musicians' Khan," or "Inn." Mohammedan troubadors from Istanbul, Cairo and Baghdad used to come here to stay for a while, trading their troubled sweet urban melodies in a delicious province. They roomed along the upper tier of the court; their camels were stabled below. The stars blazed down upon a charmed scene here; a thousand and one Arabian nights. There was dancing in the courtyard under the moon, to flute notes and lute notes raining from above, sifting down from all around. And now? Everywhere green creepers dewed with tiny white star flowers are tracing out the dust where once upon a time so many silken slippers pressed and passed.

A lone sparrow softly and silently appears. He hops about, pecks here and there, pauses—listening. Listening for what? The twilight tucks its silken coverlet about the quiet dusk, the twinkling flowers. The sparrow keeps on listening. Perhaps he can hear insects beyond our range? Or else it is the silvery dripping of the tap onto mossy stone. Or lost flute notes and lute notes alighting here and there? Or his own beating heart, perhaps? He flutters for a moment, taking a dust bath. Now he flies away.

All ancient peoples pondered the far-out folk dancing of the stars and also the chorusing birds close by. The birds did speak, in song and in the manner of their flight, to men who understood such things. Flummery of course occurred. Wisdom also flew in here and there. A feather weighs much to a fool—or to a genius. Pure chance so often triggers decisions which the mind has been preparing unbeknownst to itself.

Once, at the very moment when a Phoenician fleet offered battle to Alexander the Great, an eagle alighted on the shore behind his ships. Overjoyed at such an omen, the Macedonians howled for combat. Alexander, however, refused to commit a single vessel. "The eagle," he explained, "came down ashore." Soon afterwards he disbanded his fleet and turned inland his spear-crested torrent of men. The sense of welcome need not be a soft, or softening, thing. It strikes fine fires from the truly hard. Force of arms was only half of Alexander's strength. The other half was that he felt himself welcomed, in small things and large. Welcomed by eagles, cities, his pillow, the new day, Alexander moved easy, yet with tremendous passion and speed. He stirred up a minimum froth of blood; scorned revenge; made kings of former enemies. A uniquely generous conqueror, he tried to transcend conquest. The final stages of his grand campaign became an armed pilgrimage, a search for the horizon.

Passing from great splendor to something lovely and little, consider the ruby-throated hummingbird. As fierce as Alexander he is, and if a crow or a hawk presumes to approach his nest, this fiery fifteenth-of-an-ounce attacks at once. Not content with pursuit only, he will light upon the back of a champion forty times his own size, hastening it painfully away. He himself can travel almost a mile a minute. Still more amazing really is to see him rape a blossom with his hollow rapier. Just a tiny rainbow glisten upon the air, he hovers motionless beside the flower, sucking out its honey as if through a straw and meanwhile beating his wings about fifty times a second, just to stay still. But when in love the hummingbird does things that are difficult even for itself, like flying sideways, to show off.

Unrolling an old Chinese scroll, one finds feathery winged ideograms, and sometimes drawings too: cloudy rocks, benevolent dragons, and birds. Birds taken on the wing, drawn from life, not from dead bodies. The details are guessed at or ignored; the species can seldom be identified. Swallows may even resemble dolphins, pheasants may look like hares, and sparrows like thistledown. Yet the right sort of airiness is there, the inaudible music to enjoy. A sage had a problem about meditation. How is it possible, he asked, "to get into the bird-cage without setting the birds off singing?"

On full-moon nights it happens that great silent flocks of swifts go sailing above the clouds: dark lakes of slender-winged birds drifting, practically motionless, deep in silver. Pillowed wide upon the warm air which the summer earth exhales all through the night, they sleep up there.

The great and compelling secret of the classical world remains a secret to this day. Profound scholars have grown old in their efforts to unravel this mystery, which hundreds of thousands of people used to share. It concerns the initiation rites at Eleusis, near Athens. We know that the initiates were shown something terrible and strange which made them feel as if they had been reborn. In the classical age, most Athenian citizens saw this thing. Girls also were initiated. Slaves too, if they wished, and Greek-speaking barbarians. The rite was anything but exclusive. Yet the lips of all initiates were sealed, on pain of death. Nobody told what he had seen; no one wrote it down. The fear of punishment alone cannot explain this extraordinary fact. The initiation itself must have instilled eternal silence concerning the thing seen, a wordless wonder that could not be broken ever. And so the most famous and longed-for revelation of pagan times has vanished like smoke. We have not a clue what it was. But ancient art gives some indication of how it was shown. Apparently the initiate was presented with a simple basket covered by a napkin, and the napkin was folded back to reveal—the thing. What was in the basket? Classicists have suggested that it was a snake, an artificial phallus, a sacrificial knife, or even an ear of corn! None of these suggestions satisfy because they are too clearly symbols, toys. The Greeks were hardly children; no more so than we ourselves. There must have been some overwhelming actuality in the basket. Not a mere symbol to think about, but a revelation at once agonizing and glorious: something to make one shout straight out, as if plunged into the freezing waters of a totally unexpected reality. What was it?

Classical study comes up against a blank wall here. Yet surely there is a door to the mystery. It may be found elsewhere, far removed from Greece. For if the hearts of men are similar, their best secrets must be similar too. Three brief but ambiguous fables from the Orient, for example, give a triangulation of the pagan enigma:

Near the source of the Ganges is a sheltered hollow with a meadow and a clean-swept cave. At the door of the cave there is a grass mat. A yellowish old man in a saffron robe lies stretched out on the mat, tasting the mountain air. There is an empty china cup at his elbow. A climber approaches, struggling up the cliffs. He reaches the sheltered meadow; he approaches the old man. Nothing is said; nothing is not said. The climber sits and rests for a while. He feels a certain blissfulness about the place, and sympathy with the silent hermit. He must push on, to reach the peak; meanwhile he stays. A vague uneasiness steals over him. This pause is dreamlike; ought he to awaken? He shivers, and without thinking about it he speaks out loud: "How are things?" The old man briskly lifts a crooked hand, pointing overhead. A fat cloud sits above, flapping its silver cape. The climber takes that in. Then he looks again at the old man: "And how are you?" The hermit points downward this time, to the cup.

Things are fine—in nature, that is. So are the few people who recognize the fact without questioning it. So also are people who question without destroying the harmony of things. Even destructive people are empty; fine to that extent. Air enters everywhere.

Once upon a time the Emperor of China called for his Chief Butcher: "All my other servants keep requiring new working tools. Yet you have never asked for a new cleaver: why?" The Butcher knew not what to reply. The Emperor said, "Clearly there is a mystery here!" He called for a quarter of an ox, and had the man dissect it in his presence. The cleaver flashed and fishtailed like a happy thing, light as air. The work was very soon done; the blade remaining as sharp as before. "You have a magic cleaver!" the Emperor decided. Yet the Butcher denied it. The Emperor crossly sent for the remaining three-quarters of the ox. He caused a bright new cleaver to be brought and presented to the Butcher: "Now fall to and carve once more, as if your life depended on it!" The Butcher obeyed. The work went as well as ever; and this blade also kept its perfect edge. The Emperor withdrew his hands from his sleeves: "With my own eyes I see you cutting up the carcass, and yet—" He waved his fragile fingernails.

The Butcher prostrated himself: "I have cut nothing, O Celestial One! Beginners may do so, not your servant. I merely separate."

The third tale concerns a stone monkey who seems almost a Chinese caricature of Mithra, the Persian savior-god. Mithra was born from a living rock in the shade of a fig tree by a river. Right away, he wrestled the sun into orbit. Then he seized the shining horns of the Bull of Heaven. The great beast trampled, gored and dragged the god bumping down the long, long staircases of the stars; it was a terrible struggle. At last Mithra succeeded in slitting the bull's throat, and the world of living things poured into being on the dark tide of blood. So much for Mithra. Here, in a version delightfully translated by Arthur Waley, is how Monkey was born:

There was a rock that since the creation of the world had been worked upon by the pure essences of Heaven and the fine savours of Earth, the vigour of sunshine and the grace of moonlight, till at last it became magically pregnant and one day split open, giving birth to a stone egg . . . Fructified by the wind it developed into a stone monkey, complete with every organ and limb. At once this monkey learned to climb and run; but its first act was to make a bow towards each of the four quarters. As it did so, a steely light darted from this monkey's eyes and flashed as far as the Palace of the Pole-Star. This shaft of light astonished the Jade Emperor.

Monkey grew up comic in spirit and terrible in power. The time came when he even defied the Jade Emperor, offering to fight for the celestial throne. Monkey paid for this impertinence. He was imprisoned in an alchemical set. But his forty-nine-day cooking only hardened him; he came out more defiant still. Then the Buddha of the Western Gates made him a sporting proposition: "I will take you up in my hand. If you can leap off it, the heavenly empire is yours." Monkey knew how to ride the cloud-trapeze. Putting his cudgel behind his ear he crouched now on Buddha's palm and lightly rocketed straight up, invisible for speed. To make good his leap he kept on and on and on, until he came to a great mountain in the sky. Five rosy pinnacles shone above the clouds. And Monkey, hardly out of breath, exulted: "Here I am at the edge of the world." He made a magic ink-brush and scribbled a boast upon the rock. Irreverently, he peed. Then plunging gaily back to Buddha's palm, he claimed his reward. Buddha smiled: "Just look down." Monkey peered down with his fiery, steely eyes, and there at the base of the middle finger of Buddha's hand he saw written: *The Great Sage Equal to Heaven Reached this Place.* From the fork between the fingers arose the odor of monkey urine.

The mind can outrace daimonic forces. Imagination encompasses action, as Air does the rolling Earth. Words with thoughts even to heaven go. As for pagan Eleusis, it may be reached as well by way of China as of Banbury Cross.

There are yet more clues to what was shown at Eleusis. "Hear the voice of the reed, complaining of separations." With this handful of words, like seeds in a fountain of flute notes, a masterpiece of Moslem literature begins. Jelalludin Rumi welcomes the flute as a fellow sufferer, a reed torn from Earth and Water, separated from its whispering brothers, and cruelly lopped and pierced, martyred to make separate notes for the song's sake. Again its music fountains, like the lullaby of some lost, obedient bird, or air that speaks. The flute alone would tell us, if it could, what was in the basket at Eleusis. . . . Yet perhaps one last intimation is called for, a final hint, offered by the American Indians of the Northwest. When a Tlinkit boy made ready to become a brave, the men took him deep into the forest for a night ceremony. In the midst of the drumming and dancing round the campfire, masked figures of the gods appeared. Seizing the boy they carried him deeper still into the wilderness, away from all he knew. At dawn they halted, surrounded their shivering captive, removed their masks, and told him something never to be repeated, on pain of death. It was the most precious possession of the tribe, the Indians' best and best-kept secret: *There is no Secret.*

There is no secret unless one keeps it. No wisdom unless one acts upon it. No grownups unless one grows up. No magic words unless one speaks them. No comforter unless one gives comfort. No love unless one loves. There is only the swirling world and the still self, and a single life—one's own—stretched out between the two. These cold facts of the human condition can be very terrible and hard to face at first. Yet if only the right preparations have been made for receiving the truth, it promises a better and happier life. One becomes wiser at once, because awakened.

Imagination, startled into wakefulness, perceives that reality is not all solid by any means. And confidently steps out over the abyss.

When they folded back the napkin from the basket at Eleusis, what stood revealed? Air.

In early morning, when the lighthearted birds are at their hungriest, the earthworms come wending up for air. Thus the ground surrenders a small army to the sky. Robins, for instance, devour many times their own weight every day, and still they keep on flying. But meanwhile why should earthworms invite destruction so? Darwin noticed this enigma, and he struggled with it, but to no avail. It is one of many such problems which show "natural selection" to be one-sided. The fact is that natural sacrifice plays as great a role. The clue to the balance of nature is really: Eat and Let Eat.

Obviously we too are part of nature's balance. The worms will have our bodies—if all goes well! Yet a man is not a worm; a worm is not a bird. Something about us neither eats nor is eaten. It relates to the physical, but cannot be laid hold of in physical terms. Some say it must be infinite; others maintain that it is nothing in itself. The contradiction is meaningless, however. Why apply ideas of extension? One simply cannot measure a person's nonphysical aspect. It remains a mystery, different in kind from all directly ascertainable things. Religious people call it the soul, and they say it can be measured after all. But only in the sense of being weighed or judged by God at the world's ending. That is a matter of faith, naturally. Most ancient Greeks assumed, as the Hindus still do, that soul is air. Faith again. All based however on the realization that something about us is present yet apart, everywhere and nowhere, playing in and around and through us like the air we breathe.

Breath is the guest of breathing things. Is the soul also a guest? The Orphics, the Neo-Platonists and many Christians have said

"No." They call the soul a prisoner of the body, temporarily trapped in solid flesh. If this be true, then one's instinctive sense of welcome meets a serious check. Prisoners don't feel welcome, and according to this view the soul ought not to feel welcome upon Earth. So Earth becomes a "valley of tears." I find that a dreary idea, though better men than I am say it's all right. Nobody denies, however, that the whole concept of soul has gotten barnacled with conflicting dogmas in the course of centuries. This makes the word contentious in very many quarters.

Science-minded people prefer the term "intelligence." And some of these too believe it is basically weighable. Take I.Q. tests. But such tests only give rough estimates of the data to which a given mind has interior access. They tell nothing, except by implication, about the mind itself. Electroanalysis? We do have devices for graphing the electric charges produced by unspoken thoughts and feelings. But those electric charges also are side-effects. The electroencephalograms of Beethoven and Billy the Kid—both emotional fellows—might look alike. One's own thoughts might fly away to China or Andromeda Nebula without producing so much as a jiggle on the wire. If the immaterial part of a person merely reacted to things, then it could be tested directly. But it does so much more. It keeps moving constantly, soaring far over the fences of space and time. Its proper sky, in fact, is just what mathematicians call "the space-time continuum." The immaterial "I" can encircle the globe with the speed of light. It plays from point to point in space time at will. So long as one feels well, that is. A toothache can bring it straight home to one's head in a hurry. Then as soon as the pain stops, off it goes again: to Cousin Bill's, a dialogue of Plato's, a domestic problem, an island in the memory, a ship, a song, a dream, a dread event. Home it comes again in moments of pain. And of pleasure too. But this nonmaterial "I" is more like an intermittent guest than a prisoner.

A man may be a victim of circumstance, a clod, a drudge,

caught amongst cold folk. Worse still, he may himself prove incapable of loving, and therefore unloved. But what about his pilgrim self, the part that does soar, what will it find true in the world? Does our inborn sense of welcome correspond to what we all, as sometime pilgrims, know? It does appear that people at their best give welcome to a fellow man. Also that nature welcomes him; she does everything to welcome him. It seems clear too that death makes welcome possible. Finally, the immaterial part of a person also is welcomed. Not just in the body. Imagination gets the keys to the city of space time as well.

Sailors in the Antarctic still take special comfort from the wanderer albatross. Whoever slays him is inviting shipwreck, they say. Legend holds that the murderer himself will be condemned to roam the earth in torment, like Coleridge's Ancient Mariner. A majestic twelve-foot wing span makes the wanderer albatross Lord of Storms. Riding the gale wind he goes from horizon to horizon in minutes. He will roam thousands of miles in a week's time. He sleeps upon the deep, tempest-cradled. Some say he dozes on the wing as well. Suddenly the albatross comes back to stay with you, guiding your ship to safety through the heaving, freezing frenzy of his own home latitudes. Benignly, like a vision of a wide-sailed clipper ship, he skims the swirling mist. Yet should this good spirit chance to light upon your deck, he will prove as helpless as a paper kite—unable to launch himself clear of the ship's railings. Of all birds the greatest aloft and the least on solid ground, the wandering albatross resembles—each man's intermittent guest, or pilgrim self.

But wait—"least on solid ground." That has an ominous ring. Are all our flights, then, flights of fancy after all? Whenever we get away from objective facts, are we more or less dreaming? This question hardly ever arose until the modern age. It is insistent now, all right. And millions of people answer yes, only objective, tangible facts are real. In effect they deny reality to the albatross until it's helpless, or dead . . . hung about their necks!

This strange denial springs, it seems, from an accident of history. It is an unfortunate side-effect of scientific progress. Modern science got its first big push, as everybody knows, when it developed certain very crude but effective criteria of objectivity. Philosophers were awed by these. So were most thinking people. Thereafter, philosophy became a Game of Doubts, and our best minds appeared the most uncertain. Facts kicked up a howling storm. Imagination sank to the gray hungry waves.

The atmosphere of doubt which science stirred up in non-scientific fields was bound to sweep back upon science itself. It has happened that the most exquisite experiments turned out to "prove" the truth of something utterly false. Mountains of accumulated data rise and vanish like the mist. Mirages may appear in microscopes, and telescopes take a tendentious turn. Science, devoted to truth, keeps correcting itself as it grows. Even contradicting itself; this is inevitable. And so it comes about that the criteria of objectivity, the very foundations of science, have been shaken and are being rebuilt. But science has been profiting from these upheavals. It still races ahead.

Cracked plaster facts are chipped away, frescoes falling everywhere. Instead we see archways of creative mathematics, half-domes of daring, difficult theory. Science bursts at last into a kind of music, a longing, an echo of Nature's hidden harmony:

> *Could I revive within me*
> *Her symphony and song,*
> *To such a deep delight 'twould win me,*
> *That with music loud and long,*
> *I would build that dome in air,*
> *That sunny dome! those caves of ice!*

The new scientific spirit recalls that of the ancient Greeks. Like theirs, it verges on philosophy. Moreover it dares do just what it frightened philosophy out of doing. That is, create world-pictures. Fallible ones of course, because we are fallible. Not just the scientists, or the philosophers, or the theologians, or the poets, or whom you like, but every one of us is and always will be thoroughly fallible. Only the graceful acceptance of this truth will enable us to get together—and keep our differences—under one sky.

WONDER ON PARNASSUS

APHRODITE, GODDESS OF LOVE, used to renew her own virginity simply by sea-bathing. Proteus, the Old Man of the Sea, had a better trick yet; he could change his shape any time, more easily than changing clothes. Proteus would reveal his secrets only to the hero who caught and held fast his iridescent and elaborately mutable limbs. . . . Nonsense? But what about these modern beliefs? Astrophysicists relate that our life-giving sun renews its virginity also, by dint of a circular chain reaction. Every nucleus of carbon and nitrogen in the sun returns to its pure state once in five million years. Meanwhile, microphysicists have stumbled on a Proteus of the subatomic sea. This unknown power takes the form of infinitesimal particles which exist for just a microsecond or so before glimmering off into something else.

Any faith—religious or scientific or what you will—has two main parts. It is a "certainty" resting on a "mystery." Paradoxical, in a word. Yet without faith a man could hardly exist. Most of the time we must act, obviously, not on what we really know but on faith. Only the other fellow's faith seems paradoxical, perhaps. This makes faith a hard subject to talk about softly.

Dividing the thing into its main components is no help. "Certainties" in themselves are just too inflexible—and "mysteries" too unfathomable—for polite discussion. Around the edges, faiths often look more like hates. Yet new faiths must always arise, it seems; the kettle keeps on boiling—boiling over, too. In our own time even materialistic dogmas are matters of faith, and no less intense for that either. Is there really no general clue? Doesn't all faith relate somehow to the same human adventure?

The human adventure is also a certainty resting on mystery; faith reflects it to that extent. Faith and life alike are paradoxical. There is no solution to the paradox either. No, there is none. Except inside a person. An individual sometimes resolves the paradox inside himself. Like an electric charge, the wonder in him flashes from mystery to certainty and back again without a break. Wonder is the unifying field of mystery and certainty, faith and life. But of all human senses, the sense of wonder is the most elusive now.

People even feel ashamed of it, as if the sense of wonder were something childish or old-fashioned. This crippling shame comes partly from officious educational practice. Take away a child's books of mythology and fairy stories—force him to consult an encyclopedia instead—and first-frost bites his mind. Having been barred from the wonder of faraway things, he may later fail to find it even in things near at hand. To such a sufferer, science and philosophy will seem as dry as chalk.

Aristotle argued that men were first led to study these things, "as indeed they are today, by wonder. At first they felt wonder about the more superficial problems: afterwards they advanced gradually by perplexing themselves over greater difficulties . . . Now he who is perplexed and wonders believes himself to be ignorant. Hence even the lover of myths, in a sense, is a philosopher. For myth is a tissue of wonders." With that and no more for an introduction, let us mount the shoulder of Parnassus, to Delphi. Here myth first merged into philosophy. Here Man found his feet. Here wonder rests and grows, and the air itself is singing still.

There used to be a dragoness at Delphi, in a measureless cavern underneath the mountain: a slime-scaled monster, steaming, yet cold of breath. Whoever met her would be swept away doomed. Until at last the sun-god Apollo came and shot a strong arrow into her. Then she writhed shrieking through the forest, gasping out her life. Sunshine rotted Pytho (or *Typhaon* for typhus). She was a pollution. Yet where she died sprang forth the cold Castalian spring, clearest and lightest of waters, lovely to drink. By the side of this spring, Apollo built a temple and a shrine for the whole Greek world.

High up on the mountain the pure Castalian spring still bubbles from its gorge. There on the left begins a flowery crescent slope, terraced with the floors of many vanished temples. Even the great temple of Apollo himself is only a broad marble shelf these days—awash with sunlight—sprouting a few tremendous columns. Above the ruins soar two mighty cliffs, hollowed like your hands when you drink from them. In the violet abyss at your fingertips, great eagles swing like toys. You feel lightheaded and yet in control, like a diver on his way down. The almond blossoms shake like tambourines; songbirds converge from below.

"Midway between the Atlas and the Caucasus peaks," Delphi was long considered the center of the universe. A carved boulder called the *Omphalos*—Navel-Stone—at Delphi was the touchstone of classical culture. Delphi became the first great European place of pilgrimage. Men journeyed here chiefly to consult Apollo's Oracle, which "could not lie." This went on for a whole millennium. Every syllable uttered within the inmost shrine stood charged with significance. History, of individuals and of nations too, was created and revealed here constantly.

In ancient times, those who wished to consult the Oracle began by washing themselves in the Castalian spring. No superstition, wishful or otherwise, clouded this simple rite. Where the spring fountained forth, a welcome and a warning stood carved upon the rock. The inscription was completely free from cant, yet resonant: nothing wishy-washy. Thus it set the tone for what would follow. Freely translated (by A. J. Butler) it runs:

Come pure in heart before this hallowed fane,
Your hands fresh sprinkled with the fountain spray:
Few drops the good need; but a foul soul's stain
All ocean's water shall not wash away.

After purification there might be some days' wait. Even weeks on occasion. The questioner could grow acquainted with the place, and revel in its loveliness. The terraced slope held more— and more beautiful—Greek art and architecture than the whole world keeps today. Yet nature also met the pilgrim at each portico: sky, mountain, stream, and the valley of silvery olives gleaming far below. In this atmosphere, at once exalted and relaxed, there was casual conversation to be had with priests and fellow pilgrims. Important bits of talk doubtless reached, and influenced, the Oracle. Everything contributed, this being Delphi.

The whole place was felt to move and breathe as one being.

At last the day came when you were invited down into the sanctuary. A small room it was, with a priestess sitting there cross-legged on a high three-legged stool. She appeared to be in some sort of trance. (Authorities differ on how deep a trance this was, and nobody can say exactly how it was induced.) Suddenly she lifted up her voice. It was Apollo's voice that spoke, answering your question. The attendant priests would write her answer down if you desired it. And that was all.

The very simplicity of the thing is baffling. Because Delphi's recorded history could not be more glorious. Hundreds of inscriptions support, century by century, the legend that she was infallible. Some scholars simply throw up their hands and dismiss the great mass of her spectacular successes as post-facto forgeries —fake I-told-you-so's. This is convenient but unlikely: "You can't fool all the people all the time." Other historians have suggested that the Oracle's secret lay in mental telepathy or even clairvoyance. But that sort of "extrasensory perception" is sporadic and uncontrollable at best, so Delphi's reputation for consistency excludes it.

The real secret lies in the riddling nature of the Oracle's responses. They left a wide margin for error, but that is not the main point. They opened up the same margin for the sense of wonder to fill. The Oracle of Apollo always spoke in "certainties" but at the same time her words always pointed to the underlying mysteries of existence. So the eternal paradox of faith— certainty resting on mystery—seemed resolved at Delphi in some very direct way. Men left Apollo's presence with their confidence and wonder both renewed. Besides this, the pilgrim often went away with some strange prophecy ringing in his ears, something that he himself was supposed to bring about. The more he turned the riddle over in his mind, the more it would become involved with his own deepest instincts and desires. Until, at the decisive moment, the riddle re-emerged as a life-changing vision. By acting on it then, he could move mountains.

We all go net-fishing, let's say, on the high seas of experience. Our nets are woven of common sense, mainly. We cast them and haul them, learning much. Our main catch will be facts, of course. But then sometimes out of the darkest sea comes surging up a strange and radiant fish unlike any seen before. Our nets could never hold this one! On he comes; he may leap straight into the boat! Such are the sudden clarities that change our lives. In ancient times they surfaced very often around Delphi. The very name stands for "Dolphin," significantly enough.

Here is a typical, if slightly obvious, case of how the prophecies came true. In Delphi's earliest days there lived a young prince named Battus, who stammered terribly. Upon reaching manhood he journeyed to Delphi and begged the Oracle for a cure. Psychologists believe that stammering is caused by the unconscious fear of disappointing people. Parents who keep pressing their children to perform like adults often give stammering a start. One modern treatment is psychotherapy aimed at reconciling the stammerer to his parents, or to his memories of them. But Delphi took a more direct route. Hardly had the unhappy prince stepped down into her sanctuary than the Oracle cried: *Battus, you have come for a voice. But Apollo sends you to found a colony in Libya, rich in flocks.*

Battus choked and babbled with protest. He felt absolutely incapable of leading an expedition against hostile Africa, and he entreated the Oracle for some other word. But she would say no more. She had planted a seed; slowly the urge for high deeds grew strong in Battus. Tongue-tied though he still was, his silent heart swore to obey the god. At last he recruited a band of reckless warriors, stammered a fond farewell to his parents, and sailed away southward. It was in battle with the savage Libyan shepherds that Battus found his voice. Victorious, he then built the long-renowned Greek colony of Cyrene.

About the hardest thing to prophesy—as most men learn to their cost—is how a battle will go. After nine years before the walls of Troy, Agamemnon's best fighters had been killed, and his cause had not advanced at all. So he sent to Delphi for advice. *Conquer*, said Apollo, *by the aid of a lame prince and his mighty bow.* This encouragement contained reproof. There had been a famous archer with the host, named Philoctetes, who came down with a horrid foot infection. The Greeks had marooned him on a barren Aegean islet, simply to avoid hearing Philoctetes scream in pain. His foot soon healed, but for nine long years the prince had gone on suffering solitude, shooting sea birds for his food. Now persuasive Odysseus was sent to fetch him. After some understandably bitter hesitation Philoctetes rejoined the Argives, and became an architect of victory.

Centuries later, in historic times, Sparta inquired about Xerxes' conquering host. Grimly the Oracle responded: *For you, O dwellers in Sparta of the broad lands, either your city is sacked by Persian warriors or, not that, but you will mourn the death of a king of the line of Heracles.* The Spartan King Leonidas took this warning to heart. With his brave Three Hundred he defended Thermopylae to the death. Sparta was spared. And Leonidas had made sure that every warrior with him left a son at home.

A scholar once came to Delphi with a strange request. In the course of long and careful studies he had lost the power to laugh! And he wanted it back. The Oracle consoled him with these words: *You ask for soothing laughter, O unsoothable one. Mother at home will give it to you: pay her special honor.* So the scholar went lightly home to his mother at Metapontum, but he found nothing to laugh at there. Eventually he came to the conclusion that Apollo had been playing with him. Taking up his travels once again, he knocked glumly on about the world until he reached the island of Delos, Apollo's birthplace. There he visited the shrine of Leto, the god's mother, expecting to find an edifying statue or two as usual. Instead, the temple held only a lumpish and primitive old female idol, carved in silvery wood. The scholar laughed when he saw it.

In a moment he recalled Apollo's Oracle, and thanked the funny mother for her gift. Even the god was more down to earth than he himself had been. All brilliance, all distinction, arises from dark and obscure feelings. Knowing that, one need not trust one's own thoughts less, but enjoy them more. The useless, paralyzing awe that intellectual matters may inspire, evaporates. Two inscriptions were carved upon the sanctuary gates at Delphi: *Know Thyself* and *Nothing in Excess*. The pair constituted as liberal a moral code as ever there was. Whoever obeyed them would sin some, surely, but not forget how to laugh.

While the scholar chuckled, a whole city tried an opposite fate. A delegation of elders from Tiryns had turned up at Delphi to inquire how their town could be made serious. It appeared the folks at home laughed all the time. Hence Tiryns had forfeited its neighbors' respect; business was way off. The Oracle, presumably concealing her own smiles, prescribed a community sacrifice as the only possible cure. The whole town was to dedicate an ox to Poseidon, and throw the beast into the bay for the Earth-Shaker's private use. Slyly the Oracle added that if any man, woman or child were to laugh during this service, its whole effect would be nullified. It was.

Delphi's liberal outlook in all directions is just what makes her so especially fascinating. Her Asian and African predecessors—Uruk, Babylon, Abydos—had specialized in power, pomp, secrets, chastisements and priestly prerogatives. Delphi stayed cool. She used her own enormous magnetic attraction to combat *blind* faith at every turn. Firm prejudice and frowning solemnity were apt to be destroyed at Delphi, as often as not. In fact, Apollo here began a new game, which has been going on ever since. It is a kind of leapfrog in which wonder and intelligence play alternate roles.

Delphi was difficult to reach. But pagan pilgrims must have found delight in swinging along alone through the cool of the early summer mornings over Parnassus, bearing witness to the changing lights and sights and sounds of the new day, drawing ever closer to the unknown. Meanwhile the sun would be climbing, climbing, drawing back the string of its silver bow. By high noon the heat could burden one like an actual weight. And at that point a stranger coming from the opposite direction would be welcome indeed: a perfect excuse for turning aside together under the cool black shadow of a sycamore tree. This was the moment for breaking out the wineskin, the cheese and olives; time for warnings of robbers on the road ahead, or lions. Also talk of tolls, temples and the village girls. There might . . . Yet what if the man coming towards you had no idea of pausing even to say "Hello"? What if he came on fast, by chariot, raising a yellow thunderhead of chokeful dust about your eyes and ears, shouting, "Get off the road!"? What if he brandished his whip and cut you with it straight across the face? That is just how King Laius came at a youth named Oedipus.

The young man grabbed the whip, toppled the rude charioteer onto the highway, and killed him without a word. Small wonder! The same hot archery which purifies flowing streams can do very different things to men on the move.

Clearly, no "Oedipus complex" is needed to account for this tragedy. Yet it had been prepared in a very strange fashion. Oedipus was on his way from Delphi, where Apollo's Oracle had warned that he would kill his own father. King Laius, for his part, was hastening to the shrine in order to ask how he might avoid death at the hand of his son. The Oracle of Apollo might be dark or light, but never misty-gray. The god always prophesied action—and glorious or else grim surprise. Oedipus and Laius had never met before; never would they meet again on earth. But these angry, frightened strangers were in fact father and son.

Six hundred years before the birth of Christ, Asia Minor was called Lydia and ruled by King Croesus—the wealthiest of men. Croesus was more than a half-legendary Rockefeller or J. P. Morgan in a purple toga. He personally held the balance of power between Europe and Asia. Moreover, as a Greek-admiring and yet Oriental-style ruler, Croesus considered both continents fair game. He marched west first, grabbing the trade-rich Greek communities of the Ionian shore, along with a handful of islands on his side of the Aegean Sea. The mainland Greeks protested fruitlessly. Being disunited, poor, and across the water, they could do nothing much about Croesus' encroachments. In fact some Greeks highly approved of him as a civilizing force. Their artists and philosophers flocked to his hospitable court.

Among Croesus' visitors was Solon, the Benjamin Franklin of ancient Greece. Solon had written Athens' democratic constitution. Then, after persuading the citizens to give his laws a ten-year trial, he had abruptly exiled himself from Athens for the crucial decade. Solon's chief purpose was to disassociate his personality from the constitution and allow it to stand on its own. His secondary aim was to improve his mind at foreign courts, Croesus' included. The king treated Solon to an extended tour of the royal treasures, and then comfortably demanded: "Who is the happiest man you've ever met?" He assumed that Solon would say "Croesus," naturally. That would have been the polite and indeed expected reply for a guest at court to make. (To call an Oriental potentate unhappy, even today, is tantamount to finding serious fault with his whole kingdom.) But Solon was opposed to monarchy and addicted to truth. He gave his own harsh, solemn, forever re-echoing response: "Count no man happy, Croesus, until he be dead. Look to the end, no matter what it is you are considering. Often enough God gives a man a glimpse of happiness and then casts him to the depths."

This warning only aggravated Croesus and strengthened his resolve to keep on expanding his possessions. Having succeeded in a small way in the west, he now plotted to march eastward against Persia. However, being a careful man, he decided to first consult the famous Greek oracles about his chances of success. As a preliminary test he sent messengers to all of them with instructions to wait a hundred days and then demand to know what he himself was doing back in Lydia. In general this proved an impossible demand, as might be expected. But Delphi rose to the test. No sooner had Croesus' emissaries stepped down into her sanctuary than the Oracle sang out:

> *I count the grains of sand on the beach and measure the sea;*
> *I understand the speech of the dumb and hear the voiceless.*
> *An aroma has come to me, of hard-shelled tortoise*
> *Boiling and bubbling with lamb's flesh:*
> *The cauldron is of bronze, and of bronze the lid.*

Boiled lamb and tortoise was just what Croesus had chosen for lunch on the date of the test-question. An odd, unappetizing dish it must have been, too. Moreover, his kitchen was whole weeks away from Delphi. How the priestess knew what he was about has ever since remained a mystery. Croesus, for one, was thoroughly convinced that the sun-god, who sees all, spoke through her lips. Accordingly he at once dispatched a tribute to Delphi which included, among other things:

Item: One hundred and seventeen gold ingots.

Item: A golden image of a lion, weighing five hundred and seventy pounds.

Item: A life-size golden statue said to represent "the girl who baked his bread" (probably the temple euphemism for his favorite bride).

Item: An immense mixing bowl of purest gold, weighing a quarter-ton.

To this unprecedented treasure Croesus added an almost equal weight of silver. But gold was considered especially appropriate for the sun-god. The scientists of the time affirmed that Apollo himself took a hand in creating gold, by impregnating dull rock with fires from the sun. The king firmly believed that he could win the god to his side by returning some of this magical stuff to Delphi. He had heard that Apollo's Oracle occasionally misled lesser men by means of ambiguous responses. Croesus' lavish offerings were partly designed to forestall that sort of thing. He wanted clear answers, and he got them, too.

From a worldly point of view also, his golden gifts made good sense. Banks had not yet been invented; foreign credit was unknown. How was Croesus, plotting against Persia, to secure his rear in Greece? His tribute to Apollo was the best method available. He knew it would be prominently displayed in the Delphic treasury. He had reason to hope that such conspicuous piety would make friends and influence Greeks, and so it did. The Greek city-states hastened to make peace with generous Croesus. Sparta even went so far as to ally herself with him.

Through the mouth of the Oracle, Apollo now assured Croesus' emissaries that if the king marched against Persia he would cause the downfall of a mighty empire. So Croesus gleefully set about levying troops. To pay them he struck gold and silver coins. Some Ionian princes before him had tentatively minted electrum, a silver and gold alloy, but Croesus is generally credited with being the father of modern coinage. He put it on a grand scale. Croesus was the first to wield a mercenary army, too. Previous troops had fought either for home and country or for board and booty, whereas his soldiers fought for cash. He now sent a second present to Delphi, consisting of gold coins for every priest and citizen there. The Delphians in turn voted to give the king and all his people honorary citizenship in their sacred town. The god was with him; the Greeks were for him; his troops were fat and fierce. Victory beckoned, open-armed, from the East. Croesus marched, and got smashed.

The Persian king, whose name was Cyrus, had Croesus chained

atop a huge pyre in his own courtyard, to be burned as a public spectacle. The pitchy faggots were lit; the fire crackled thirstily. Then, as the smoke began to lick about his ankles, Croesus was heard to cry out three times, in anguish of spirit: "Solon! Solon! Solon!"

By rights, the story should have ended there. But Croesus' thrice-repeated cry piqued the Persian's curiosity. Cyrus sent heralds near the fire to demand who or what had been invoked. After some hesitation, the doomed and writhing king told of Solon's warning, which he himself had so conspicuously failed to heed. "I would give all my gold," he added ingenuously, "that other rulers might receive the benefit of Solon's advice." Just at that moment, a violent thunderstorm broke overhead, quenching the murderous flames. Whether Cyrus was the more impressed by this seeming sign from heaven or by Croesus' new-found wisdom is uncertain. In any case he had Croesus released and brought to sit beside the throne.

Herodotus relates that Cyrus made much of the singed and shivering Lydian, "gazing upon him with a sort of wonder, as did everyone else who was near enough to see." After a time, Croesus humbly inquired what Cyrus' troops might be doing at the moment. "Sacking your city," the Persian replied. "No," said Croesus, "they are sacking yours." Cyrus, struck by the good sense of this remark, immediately appointed Croesus to be his own grand vizier. Absolute despots can afford dramatic gestures which a minute can reverse. "Ask what you will of me," Cyrus added magnanimously, gesturing in the direction of what had been Croesus' treasury. But the new vizier's one request was bitterly modest. He begged permission to send his own burning-chains as a final and ironic offering to Delphi, with just one more question for the Oracle: "Is it Apollo's custom to cheat his benefactors?"

Gods are not so easily embarrassed. Apollo granted a twofold reply: First, no man escapes his destiny. Second, Croesus should have asked which empire he was destined to destroy—the Persian, or his own.

Croesus himself had the gall to tell Cyrus: "No one is fool enough to choose war instead of peace, because in peace sons bury their fathers, whereas in war fathers bury their sons." But gold and greed together had, like mischievous elves, drawn the proud Lydian on to deathly war. Apollo must have smiled to see so wishful and so busy a truth-seeker fail. Croesus' first mistake was to consult the Oracle through messengers. Had he been on the spot himself, the crucial follow-up question might well have popped into his head. His second mistake was in making up his mind beforehand, so that the god's response came to him colored by the blood in his eye already. Bright treasure in the hands of a bloody-minded man will always generate dark powers, whether for or against himself.

Croesus' golden gifts had helped confirm Delphi's ascendancy as the hearthstone of Greek culture. This drew together and enriched the whole Greek world. With Lydia destroyed, the Persian emperors now became aware of Greece for the first time, and vowed to take it. Thus the stage had been set for the first great struggle between East and West—at Marathon. The human adventure, like the gold of Croesus, found its new home in Europe.

Once a stranger sailed alongside an island fishing boat and offered the men a high price for whatever might be in their net. Delighted, they sealed the bargain. The net then proved to contain a poor catch of fish—and a great golden tripod beautifully made. The stranger, who was from Ionia, held the islanders to their pact. But they resented it. War ensued. Both sides had a case in this conflict, yet neither could win, so they asked Delphi to arbitrate. The Oracle responded: *Whoever is first of all in wisdom, to him the tripod belongs.*

At that time the wisest man alive appeared to be Thales, the

Ionian scientist. Peace was declared and the tripod presented to him. But Thales immediately passed the tribute on to a second sage as being much wiser than himself. The other passed it on in his turn. And so the prize made the rounds of seven great sages, returning at last to Thales. Thereupon he dedicated it to Apollo at Delphi. All seven sages found this appropriate because wisdom appears from the deep—as had the golden tripod—or from above like sunshine, and returns whence it came.

The story of the golden tripod may have legendary overtones. There is nothing legendary about Delphi's making of another sage about a century later. Impressive though he seemed to his companions, Socrates in middle life had not yet consulted his own secret heart, or the hearts of his fellows either. Then one day a disciple of his who happened to be passing through Delphi impulsively stopped there and inquired of the Oracle: "Is any man wiser than Socrates?" Her answer was brief and to the point. The young traveler was careful to have the priests record it in writing. Then he hurried home and gave Socrates the Oracle's reply: *No man*. Although renowned for his perfect calm in battle, Socrates trembled like a coward now. The news appalled him. It so happened that the jury which later condemned him to death (for "teaching impiety") heard the rest of this tale from Socrates' own lips:

> *I said to myself, "What can the god mean? What is the interpretation of his riddle? For I know that I have no wisdom, small or great. What then can he mean when he says I am the wisest of men? And yet he is a god, and cannot lie." After long consideration I . . . reflected that if only I could find a man wiser than myself, then I might go to the god with a refutation in my hand. [To find somebody wiser] I went to one man after another, being not unconscious of the enmity which I provoked. And I lamented and feared this, but necessity was laid upon me. The word of*

God, I thought, should be considered first. And I said to myself, Go I must, to all who appear to know . . . I will tell you the tale of my wanderings—my "Heraclean Labors" as I may call them—which I endured only to find at last the oracle irrefutable. [What it meant was] 'The man is wisest who, like Socrates, knows that his wisdom is in truth worth nothing!'

A man like Socrates sits far down the table at the feast of life. He asks for little; yet his modest bowl gleams like the full moon, his spoon becomes the sparkling Big Dipper and his glass bursts into cool, hovering flame. The mysteries around him are his meat and drink. He sings their praise; thus he gives meaning to the feast. And always such a man drinks to mankind, though he drink hemlock.

The citizens of Delos once sent a delegation of suppliants to Delphi. Their island was having a long run of inexplicable bad luck, and they begged Apollo for a remedy. Easily found, said the Oracle. They need only double the size of their chief temple at home! So the islanders set to work with a will. Soon they had exactly doubled their temple's length, width and height. Where-upon their troubles also multiplied. Confusion reigned, and with it some regret. Delphi's full glory was already on the wane at that time. The island's bright young men eventually formed a second delegation to a different sort of shrine: Plato's brand-new Academy at Athens. The philosopher elected to receive them in his garden; he listened with care; he agreed that times had changed. Intellectual adventure was in the air now. One really should try to keep up with things. The Oracle had told them specifically to double their temple, but they had made it eight times larger!

Plato then led his inquirers to the same garden gate by which they had entered, and said goodbye. Circling the Academy building, they may have noticed the inscription over the front door: *You cannot enter here unless you know geometry.*

The fact is that Greek philosophy and science both mirrored the spirit of Delphi. Their main effort also was to build reasonable certainties upon the deeps of mystery. In philosophy of course they succeeded to an amazing degree. In theoretical science, less so. But at least three ancient Greek models of the universe still remain in dispute. Why? Because each was so firmly based upon a mystery which endures.

Empedocles of Acragas, to start with, saw that Earth, Air, Fire and Water are continually mingled and separated out again. They play into each other, said Empedocles, like the colors on an artist's palette. Love and hate command them. This second half of Empedocles' theory remains a passionate concern to science. For "love and hate" we substitute two pairs of terms: attraction-repulsion and cohesion-disorder. But the general meaning is the same and the mystery still present. Of course these forces are intimately bound up with gravity, electromagnetism and spin, but what are the secrets of their cosmic interplay?

After Empedocles, Anaxagoras shocked patriotic Athens by confessing that he himself felt "most at home in the night sky." That's wonder for you. He also announced, at the risk of his neck, that "the sun is just a great molten rock." Anaxagoras went on to explain eclipses, comets and meteors correctly, but by then almost nobody was listening. This father of astronomy had a wondering eye for the microcosm as well. Mere mingling of the elements was not enough, he thought. Something more would be required to produce individual life and order. So he posited the existence of tiny, invisible "seeds" within all things. He was half right. Inorganic matter can do without the seeds of Anaxagoras— which we call "chromosomes"—but every living thing requires them. Each human adult carries in himself about a thousand billion double sets of these neat little items—weighing perhaps two ounces for the lot. They are small. In fact, on such a minute level you generally find complete confusion, with atoms bounding and rebounding randomly. Yet somehow each single chromosome not only maintains itself in good order but also stores and transmits the plans and building-code for the entire body. So Anaxagoras, like Empedocles, did put his finger on a most mysterious Something, or combination of Somethings, which has yet to be explained.

When and if the budding of life is explained, science will almost certainly be "revolutionized" again. Henri Bergson, who entered the problem from the philosophical side, gives its tender mystery in a minimum of words. Life, he once wrote, "requires the least possible room at the start, a minimum of matter, as if the organizing forces only entered into space with regret."

Like pulling a dragon from a thimble, Democritus of Abdera uncorked the boldest reduction of all. "In truth," he announced, "there are only atoms and the void!" Democritus' own word *atomoi* meant "uncuttables." Therefore, since we have smashed the atom we retain a misleading term for it. Democritus himself never ventured to suggest a size-limit for this silvery spinning lure. He could not have dreamed that it might one day be put to the test. His own point was purely theoretical. He meant that at bottom there must be some sort of building blocks, and space to build in, and *nothing else*. With one leap, he brought "scientific objectivity" to its ultimate. Democritus fathered materialism. After twenty-five centuries the excitement and mystery have yet to ebb out of this building-block conception, yet it has been shaken by a new development. The infant science of wave mechanics is uncovering weird uncertainties at the subatomic level. Down there where nucleons, electrons and neutrinos dance together—weaving tiny fairy rings—you get a kind of radiance which defies measurement. To measure a whole ocean is possible, but the shimmer of a solitary sunbeam on a wave . . . ?

What Democritus assumed must be uncuttable is really immeasurable, twinkling its welcome like some infinitely distant star. That makes it less *and* more than a material thing. No better proof could be required of the fact that science still is building on the deeps of mystery, just as in Democritus' own day.

There is a tiny spider which voyages upon the winds. Late in summer he will spin a single very long filament out from himself, letting the breeze take it up. He himself goes along, eventually, like a minute tassel on a practically invisible bellpull. Arriving at last over the county, or country, of his choice, the little wanderer reefs in his thread of a sail and gently parachutes to earth. Amongst his cousins there is one who spins an airtight web anchored to plant stems well below the waters of a pond. Then he busily brings bubbles down, releasing them to swell the web from beneath. Behold, a subaqueous palanquin for all the family! The Navajo Indians still revere "Old Spider Mother" as their first teacher, the source of Man's devices. Her versatile filaments, spun from within, are so like human thought.

In fact, primitive mythologies the world over seem to have included a beneficent, instructive spider. But we have mainly late legends to show for this. The spider encourages King Alfred of England. He hides King David the Psalmist in a moment of danger. In Ovid's *Metamorphoses*, the goddess Minerva is credited with being the first and best of all weavers. However she comes into conflict with a mortal girl named Arachne, a weaver whom

> *The nymphs would often watch in wonder,*
> *Leaving their vineyards or the river waters,*
> *To see her finished work, or watch her working*
> *With such deft gracefulness. It did not matter*
> *Whether she wound the yarn in balls, or shaped it*
> *With skillful fingers, reaching to the distaff*
> *For more material, all soft and cloudy . . .*

Arachne dared challenge the goddess herself to a weaving contest, and the challenge was accepted. Minerva embroidered her tapestry with cautionary scenes: proud mortals punished and turned into animals by the gods. Arachne's voluptuous endeavor showed the same gods deceiving and seducing mortal girls. It's all in the poem, beautifully translated by Rolfe Humphries. When both tapestries were finished and spread out on the lawn for comparison, there seemed little to choose between them. As for Arachne's:

> *Neither Minerva, no, nor even Envy,*
> *Could find a flaw in the work; the fair-haired goddess*
> *Was angry now, indeed, and tore the web*
> *That showed the crimes of the gods, and with her shuttle*
> *Struck at Arachne's head, and kept on striking . . .*
> *"This punishment shall be enforced for always*
> *On all your generations." As she turned*
> *She sprinkled her with hell-bane, and her hair*
> *Fell off, and nose and ears fell off, and head*
> *Was shrunken, and the body very tiny,*
> *Nothing but belly, with little fingers clinging*
> *Along the side as legs, but from the belly*
> *She still kept spinning; the spider has not forgotten*
> *The arts she used to practice.*

In the Greek city of Thebes, early one morning, a most unusual spiderweb appeared. It was woven wide as a shepherd's cloak, banded like a rainbow, straight across the altar of Demeter, the Corn Goddess. In the way of warning or of blessing, what meant this omen? The local Oracle of Apollo gave an ambiguous response: *A web woven; a curse for one; a blessing for another.* So Thebes sent a delegation to Delphi. There the Oracle spoke clearly enough—in the light of history. Her answer seemed impenetrably dark at the time: *This the gods reveal as a token to all mortals, but most especially to the Thebans and their neighbors.*

Three months later the Macedonian prince Alexander came to

power in the north. Thebes had paid unwilling homage to his father, King Philip. This seemed the right moment to revolt. But Alexander came down upon Thebes by forced marches and crushed it utterly. Thus he spun the first home-strand of . . . what? An all-encompassing web.

About the last great individual to learn his lifework at Delphi was Diogenes—the Cynic. Young Diogenes had come specifically to ask what he should attempt in the way of a career. The Oracle cried out: *Deface the currency!* That was a poser. Back home in Sinope, Diogenes' father had been master of the mint. Father and son together had made a practice of confiscating false coins and defacing them with a cold chisel. But as so often happens, their strict performance of duty went unappreciated. In fact it brought disgrace, ruin and exile. Yet Apollo now demanded that Diogenes persist in the same course! Or was that really the idea? Diogenes thought and thought about it. Then suddenly he knew what was meant: not "currency" so much as "current ways." The god had called upon Diogenes to strike through the silver plating of society and expose the tin underneath! Here was a program close to the young man's heart.

So Diogenes became a tangle-bearded hermit in the midst of men. Dramatically swinging a lighted lantern he would stalk the daytime crowds—"Looking for somebody honest." His castle was an upended winevat by the gates of Corinth. Alexander the Great called on him there. All radiant, the Conqueror leaned down across the neck of his white charger, doffed his golden helmet and inquired what he might do for Diogenes. "Move on," Apollo's man suggested. "You're in my light."

Delphi's final riddle was fantastically appropriate. Scholars therefore suspect it. This last account may actually have been forged—or not. There is no way of telling any more. In any case the story goes that Caesar Augustus went to Delphi and asked who should succeed him as emperor. To everyone's astonishment an uncanny silence pervaded the shrine. The Oracle said nothing at all. Finally the trembling pilgrim in purple begged that she explain her silence. With that, she raised her fitfully gleaming eyes and spoke for the last time: *A Hebrew boy bids me leave this house and go to the Underworld.*

Augustus thoughtfully withdrew. He returned to Rome. And there, certainly, he did raise an altar dedicated to a nameless god.

Augustus' successors, especially Hadrian, tried hard to resuscitate Delphi, but to little avail. Julian the Apostate—the last pagan emperor—made the final attempt. His answer came not from the Oracle but from her remaining priest: *Tell the king, the fair hall is fallen to the ground. No longer has Apollo a hut, nor a prophetic laurel, nor a spring that speaks. Even the water of speech is quenched.* The center of inspiration having shifted to Palestine, Apollo's work was done—and well done too. But wonder is forever. The margin for wonder, which opened so decisively at Delphi, sparkled anew in the light of the Star of Bethlehem. Wise men have always humbly followed wonder's light.

A modern philosopher, Alfred North Whitehead, distills the whole skyful of conflicting thoughts and faiths to a single raindrop: "Philosophy begins in wonder. And at the end, when philosophic thought has done its best, the wonder remains. There have been added, however, some grasp of the immensity of things, some purification of emotion by understanding."

It happened that way at Delphi in the old days. Apollo's Oracle still speaks, in fact, for those who have ears to hear.

NIGHT AIRS

THE NIGHT ALONG MY mountainside lies quilted with sounds and silence. There is the wind in the pines like a great river meandering now slow, now still, turning back upon itself, breaking into rapids, sighing, whispering and softly roaring sometimes as it moves. Once in a great while there is rain, downrushing and then trickling, dripping, a rich and curious music of waters enveloping the slope. Sometimes in the height of summer a nightingale sings all night long nearby. Cooler weather brings the sheep down from the heights. They graze mainly by night. So out of the rain or the cloud or the dark starlit shoulder of the mountain comes an awakening medley of sheep bells. The shepherd of this particular flock buys his bells in Athens, all of hand-wrought copper and bronze. They are his one extravagance. He has nearly a hundred sheep, each gifted with its own clear bell. Some of the bells come big as beer mugs; others are as small as a baby's fist. Their notes appear as various as the patterning of snowflakes. The sound of each slides separately upon the air, now here, now there, opening like crocuses.

The shepherd has been told to stay away from the village, for fear of awakening people. But I live a little way out, and he can awaken me whenever he likes. I share his passion for the peculiar music of the bells. His sheep are swans to me, voiced like the nightingale. They improve the night. Awakening to music such as this is like dreaming, and the dreaming is like sleeping again, only better. The fountain of youth which flows more or less secretly everywhere and always, the plenitude of the depths, bubbles in this night music.

It happens that I know this shepherd's family. They have a raw little cement-block house, farther along the slope. It is their first solid dwelling, just built, and in the yard beside it stands their former home. Home? A brushwood hovel held together with baling wire. In this they raised their four lovely daughters, who are straight-backed, clear-eyed, and anything but wild. The house is more respectable and they are proud of it, like a royal family showing off the palace. Their next step will be a little store, perhaps. The shepherd's wife speaks shyly and yet firmly of this. Why not give up sheep-herding and move closer to town? There is more money to be had in selling meat than in keeping animals. The girls must learn embroidery; weaving is too coarse work for them. They need husbands with shoes, not silly sheep loaded with bells. She hates the music of the bells, which her own husband so loves. She too has a dream, and she has been through quite a lot. She may yet have her way. The shepherd feels the likelihood of this. He laughs uneasily, turns vague, calls his dog and wanders off along the ridge. Whatever must be must be. Yet for the present at least the mountain belongs to him. It is a noble mountain.

To harvest the sounds of the night, one may not think. So I try to put the shepherd from my mind. His days are numbered; I will see him no more. Neither the happy, troubled shepherd nor his sheep, hung with bells. The sheep go nibbling along, their wool dewy with starlight. They are thin-shanked bundles, greedy feeders, their voices urgent and mild. Now and again the shepherd whistles to the dog that nips them. He whistles sharp and clear: an icicle of sound. Then sometimes he makes a deep vibrating noise through his lips, speaking sheep's language. They say he plays a reed pipe also, but I am not sure of this, and something has prevented me from asking him. What sounds like man-made music may be just a singing in my own mind; or else accidental melodies which leap like salmon through the cool cascading chaos, the turbulent Milky Way, of the bells.

> *Most heavenly music!*
> *It nips me into listening, and thick slumber*
> *Hangs upon mine eyes: let me rest.*

I must have been sleeping, but now the boisterous yipping and tumbling of a dog pack yanks me awake once more. The noise bowls along the lane to my gate, and stops. Are they investigating the garbage can? I await the faint clang of it hitting the ground. But no, some other interest—a stray cat perhaps—has drawn them off downhill to the left. They are into the woods now, padding along in silence. My own spotted hound rises from the hearth and shakes himself, flapping his soft ears. Now he must be lying down again, curled the other way. He gives a snuffling sigh. From the valley comes the thrumming of the Athens-Salonica train. A neighbor's goats are devouring my back fence in the dark: the black mother flanked by two snowy-white kids. I can hear their gentle *eh-eh-eh-eh*. Now comes a single shrilling cry: it was the little owl of Athena, winging by.

A heavy truck in low gear groans along the road below. Bringing oak timber from the north, perhaps. As is the custom here on clear nights, the truck shows no lights. And I too am traveling without lights, voyaging although motionless; driving with no hands or wheels; stretched out in the same general direction as the highway. I feel a sort of oneness with things going on. Instead of stopping at my ears they seem to ease all through the empty spaces of my body, flowing through and over me as they are flowing through the pines and over the mountain. The night sounds belong to the air, to the mountain, and to me. Our three worlds merge.

Now the wind shifts and I hear the sheep bells once again for a moment, very far off. They create a natural music, so to speak, no more frozen into pattern than the wind itself. Floating among the curling, twining breezes of this music, I find myself daydreaming of Chinese wind bells. Also the huge sculptured bells in Oriental rain temples. Such bells were clapperless; they never rang to make the stars speed up the dance of night nor cloud dragons bump snouts on the cold moon . . .

Again the owl's cry! He must have passed quite near the house this time, on silent wing. He has gone. The good sounds of the night give meaning to the silences, as the owl's fierce cry accents his utterly silent flight. He hoots to frighten mice, frogs and snakes into betraying themselves by some tiny movement. And he flies silently in order to hear them twitch. There will be no more sleep for me tonight; I let silence sink into my thoughts. Silence of sleeping songbirds. Of heavy crows huddled black in black. Silence of the waiting hare, the delicately prowling fox. A mouse discreetly works at his nest in my bookcase, with many long pauses. He listens too. We hear the very distant ghostly lowing of a cow. Silence of moths alighting here and there: moonlight's velvet paws. Near at hand a dog barking, barking, friendly, greeting some silent visitor.

Towards dawn the cock-crows like sudden spires of mica fountaining near and far. Silence of bats at work, like tiny mad umbrellas against the fading stars. Blue dawn comes, and the yellow dawn. Sputtering of a motorbike on the road. The whole garden, turning towards day, sighs out its sweetest fragrances. The crows like mournful suburbanites go flocking loudly overhead to work. Chattering of children upstairs. I sit up to see the waxy red flamelets of the pepper plant on the windowsill, and wet purple petunias moving against the green of the pines. The sparkling sprinkling of dew. Now the sleepy golden sun shoves our mountain to one side, like a pillow, as he climbs out of bed.

PART THREE

FIRE

The tremendous and yet exquisitely delicate shrine of the Egyptian sun-god's daughter, Hatshepsut. Behind the cliff lies the fabled Valley of Kings.

On the Aegean island of Mykonos, an old woman bringing incense home from church symbolizes the eternal in the fires and the questions of life.

SUN METAL

Gently curving promenades lead us under myrrh trees from the land of Punt. Here the earth is black, the grass yellow, and the sky like brass. Karnak beckons. Already you can see its crimson pennants above the palm trees. And the blinding points of two slim obelisks which outblaze even the sky. Sheathed in bright metal, they look like spears of sunlight lifted back towards heaven.

We come to the gate, a place of shadow between pylons like painted cliffs. One scene is repeated left and right in gaudy bas-relief: Pharaoh slaughtering his foes, as usual. If you slip through for a moment and peek between the swollen pillars you may see priestesses practicing a dance. They are virgins, white-lipped and dark-eyed, the finespun daughters of the rich, and this is their Junior League. Softly they whirl, shaking their bells, looking like fashion models except that their clothes are all right: transparent nightgowns perfuming the air. In the pool of this fountain are fish from all over the world. That path leads through a game preserve to the palace: no admittance, I'm afraid. The yacht club is over on the right. These mud walls hide grand mansions; you can hear the songbirds in the courtyards. Mind the beggar. Now we're coming to a poorer section: these people sleep six to a room, but at least they're artisans and not just slaves. Watch out for the fat scribes sweating in their litters. The dry slaves are singing of how they love to carry such masters.

We're getting close to the bazaar now: bronze trays heaped with mangoes, dates, spitted lamb, roast ducks and glistening fish of the Nile. Have you any copper hoops, or goods to trade? Too bad, for here you can get ostrich feathers and panther skins from Nubia, cedar chests and pine nuts from Lebanon, Red Sea coral, ointments of Arabia, Cretan jars, Old Kingdom statuettes that were stolen from the pyramids ages and ages since, toys, harps of gold, Syrian wine, Babylonian horses, sports chariots (very expensive), eye paint, or perhaps a roll of papyrus for your diary. Here are candy stores, swarming with bare-bottomed children and flies. Now we pass brothels, beer halls, military-surplus stores—getting close to the river. Mind your wallet; this waterfront is notorious. The granite obelisk on the barge down there came all the way from Elephantine; and how they expect to haul it up the bank I'll never know. A white-armed baker watches the kids play stickball. As you bite into his brioche, hear the little donkey's doomful bray. Quick, step aside! Chariots . . .

The many-tendriled stream dissolves in mist. Yet it was there thirty-five centuries ago, when the sun-god Ammon ruled Egypt through his daughter, Hatshepsut. Such a thing had never happened before. Hatshepsut's husband was the rightful pharaoh, and a formidable man in his own right. Yet somehow his fiery, steely bride had got the better of him. She kept him like a lion on the leash. Meanwhile she controlled the world's greatest empire absolutely and made it prosper.

For the sake of orthodoxy, Hatshepsut blandly claimed to have been born a boy. Surviving portraits show that she looked boyish, as sinuous as a length of cable, and yet lovely too. Inscriptions compared the slim tyrant to the mooring lines of a Nile vessel: *The bow-cable of the south . . . and the stern-cable of the north is she, our commanding mistress!* This is the earliest-known allusion to a "ship of state."

The world would never see so great an empress again, perhaps, until the days of England's Good Queen Bess. In some ways these monarchs resembled each other. Both dedicated their countries to precarious peace, trade, and indomitable sea power. Hatshepsut's fleets ranged the Mediterranean, of course. Also, they passed directly from the Nile into the Red Sea, by means of a canal near the Delta, to explore far down the coasts of Africa and India. From the south they came back laden with ebony, ivory, cinnamon and baboons. These last were especially valued as temple-keepers, since baboons invariably greet the sun-god Ammon in the morning with passionate acclaim.

Gold the queen required not, having plenty of that at home. Hatshepsut's hostages wore fetters of pure gold. By way of contrast her own golden bracelets and necklaces were set with tiny filings of the rarest metal in Egypt, which was iron, faceted like gems. Of an evening, her warm, dark, slender limbs would be mantled in cool cloth of gold. Her banquet tables sparkled with services of silver and gold. In the musky shadows of her boudoir, where the ferocious king entered only at Hatshepsut's bidding, gold also gleamed. Gold in its natural state is like some secret trickle of sunlight. Once refined it becomes amazingly heavy, gently malleable, ever-sweet butter from the cloudy cows of heaven. It will not rust nor tarnish, never change its own sunny nature. For all these reasons, the ancient Egyptians reverenced gold as a mineral surrogate of the sun-god above. When they called gold "the King of Metals" they meant precisely that. Just as Hatshepsut and her captive husband drew their divinity from the sun-god, so also did gold, after its fashion. Gold was the tangible essence of divine wisdom and the living proof of immortality. And Hatshepsut's first concern as queen was to protect this semimystical gold standard in the midst of Egypt's gold glut. Her second concern was to forestall the flight of Egyptian gold to other, relatively gold-starved, countries. Her third concern was to exhibit an incalculable treasure to all traders and travelers in Thebes, the nation's capital, thus proving Egypt's claim to be the wellspring of civilization and prosperity. How to accomplish these three policies?

Hatshepsut records that the answer came to her in a flash of devotion: *I sat in the palace and I remembered him who fashioned me, and my heart led me to make for him two obelisks of electrum, whose points would touch the heavens.* Accordingly she ordered that two immense granite needles, each a single block, be hewn from the quarry at Aswan. They were split off from the cliff with infinite care, and floated down to Thebes on barges. Each stood about ninety-seven feet and weighed about three hundred and fifty tons. The Queen had both needles thickly sheathed with electrum, a gold and silver alloy. Erected in Karnak Temple, they pierced the roof to dominate the whole countryside.

Surviving inscriptions tell the entire story. In passing, Hatshepsut remarks that the required gold and silver were measured out from her treasury "like sacks of grain." The twin obelisks are still to be seen at Karnak, although one has fallen over and both, of course, have lost their precious sheaths. The river of gold flows on. Winding in and out of all steel vaults and coffers, the sun metal nourishes the whole civilized world. Safe and solid though it may appear, gold is always liquid in the fourth dimension: time. It may stand very tall, or sleep well in under the roots of mountains, or slumber in shipwrecks, yet it can also crack the earth wide open or cross the ocean at a bound or fill up the cellars of a great and ephemeral city. In the depths of this fiery stream, history stands reflected forever, gleaming with weird lights. The acts of long-dead persons may reappear as crystals, rubies, amber, jade, under the flowing gold.

Passing like sunfish through a prism we come to Caribbean waters in the year 1502. The galleon below us is *Capitana*, Christopher Columbus' flagship on his fourth and final voyage to the New World. Like a pelican she scuds along, ungainly but swift. With a strong wind astern these toplofty Spanish tubs can raise up to twelve knots, amazingly enough. *Capitana* carries nine officers, fourteen old salts and no fewer than twenty beardless youths: it is balanced for adventure. This is just the kind of crew Columbus likes best. In the crises that are commonly supposed to "separate the men from the boys," he has discovered, boys often do best. The admiral in his cabin, alone as usual, sits hunched over one of the many volumes he always takes on his travels. As he reads, he feels for his quill pen and, muttering, re-underlines a word: *gold*. Always he must mark that word, in all his books; it is an obsession with him. Yet no man can accuse Columbus of personal greed. Has he not refused fat estates at home in order to follow his destiny upon the deep? Austerely to search out new lands, rich in gold, for the glory of Spain—to find gold, at the dark back of the last sunset . . . He shuts his book, rushes outside and takes his stand at the poop-deck rail, shading his eyes.

The expedition's three other caravels are all in sight, bobbing briskly along. From the helm of one, his brother Bartholomew shouts a greeting. And Columbus' own twelve-year-old son, Ferdinand, replies from a perch in *Capitana*'s rigging. All seems smooth sailing. A fearful Irish wolfhound comes bounding up the gangway to nuzzle the admiral's hand. Idly, Columbus fondles the ears of this ship's mascot. Dismissing the dog, he pulls his brown cowl over his tousled red head. The wind, getting gustier, tugs at his rough monk's habit. As a lay Franciscan brother the admiral proudly wears the uniform of the order. Humility and pride, intuition and fanaticism, energy and decay keep struggling for mastery in Columbus. At fifty-one, he is already an old man, not very far from death, yet crackling with energy and sharp commands. When he grows quiet, however, he becomes another creature: a wizened wizard of the salt-sea ways. Or in the darkest watch of night he may suddenly appear on deck hollow-eyed and crumpled, like a dry, wind-driven, scurrying leaf.

He straightens now to order the helm hard-over, setting a new tack and a new course: for Santo Domingo, chief port of Hispaniola. But why? The local governor, Ovando, despises him. His old foe with the opera villain's name, Bobadilla, is in residence there. Most important, his sovereigns, Ferdinand and Isabella, themselves have expressly forbidden Columbus to go near the island! No matter: he just crowds on more sail.

What followed this abrupt decision on Columbus' part is a chapter of history hardly equaled in the annals of romance. An oily swell, ruffled in patches by capricious winds, was rolling from the southeast. High cirrus clouds streamed swiftly aloft. Flocks of seal and manatee gamboled between the ships. The admiral's arthritis bothered him. These little signs, taken together, foreshadowed a murky, hurrying hand that becomes a black, sky-wide fist in good time and slams small ships under almost without fail. Twice before Columbus had sailed under the shadow of this thing, a force more terrible than any lords of earth.

The sun still shone when he anchored safely off Santo Domingo. Inside the harbor thirty splendid vessels lay at anchor, low in the water, loaded full of gold. The immense new wealth they carried had been extorted from the Indians for the Spanish

Court, also for Governor Ovando, Don Bobadilla—and for a handful of the humbler sort whose claims required settling. Columbus, though he could not know it, was one of these last. At the moment his own thoughts were not of gold but of death, a whole wealth of death, death for many, coming out of the sky. He penned an urgent message and sent it ashore. The governor received the message in his garden. He glanced at it. Then he surveyed the smiling blue sky overhead and felt the soft still air caress his cheek. Howling with laughter, he summoned his court to hear Columbus' latest piece of pretension. His lieutenants sputtered with merriment, tears standing in their eyes. Even stern Bobadilla hooted. The message was this: First, Columbus humbly begged shelter inside the harbor for his ships. Second, he urged that the fleet already at anchor double and triple its mooring lines. Third, he said a hurricane would strike soon.

Ovando sent answer: Columbus must sail away at once. Moreover, Bobadilla's thirty-galleon Gold Fleet was to weigh anchor also, the same hour, for Spain. And let there be no nonsense about bolts from the blue. "What man ever born, not excepting Job," Columbus wrote afterwards, "would not have died of despair when in such weather, seeking safety for son, brother, shipmates and myself, we were forbidden the land and harbor that I, by God's will and sweating blood, won for Spain!" But he obediently stood off along the coast which he himself had discovered. He found some poor shelter at a rivermouth, and anchored his tiny fleet there before dark. The hurricane struck in the night, offshore, blowing over eighty miles an hour. Their cables parted and Columbus' four little ships were scattered whirling far out over the dark sea. Yet his seasoned hands and beardless sailors, his brother and his son, all played their parts like heroes. Each ship survived, with every man aboard. In fact their adventures on this "High Voyage," as Columbus himself called it, were really just beginning.

The Gold Fleet meanwhile had sailed grandly out to sea, into the night, under the poised fist. Twenty-five proud galleons, including Bobadilla's own, went down before dawn. Only four limped back to port, sinking even as they came. One single vessel, the smallest of them all, got through to Spain. Its cargo: gold, like the rest. But with a difference: this single shipload was Columbus' personal share.

Hurricanes or no hurricanes, the New World's gold kept flowing briskly to Europe for a long time thereafter. In the long run it upset the Old World's feudal ways, helping to hasten in the modern age of big money, big industry, big cities and big wars. "This yellow slave," said Shakespeare gloomily, "will make black white, foul fair, wrong right, base noble, old young, coward valiant."

Will the sun-god's fiery metal ever cease its deep streaming about the Earth? Not likely, unless man learns to manufacture it for himself. Alchemy would make gold an ornament instead of an historic force. Its sources would be general and its flow more like an imperceptible diffusion.

Man's effort to create gold at home goes back at least as far as Queen Hatshepsut's day. Its earliest-known recipes are contained in the "Emerald Table" of an Egyptian known as Hermes Trismegistus. His dark, elaborate instructions have been augmented and perhaps confused by men of every civilized race, all down the centuries. The Arabs and Chinese proved especially enthusiastic alchemists. Medieval and Renaissance Europe were steeped in this pseudoscience. Basically, the adepts of all eras and all nations agreed that a veritable Tree of Metals grows under the earth. The fairest fruit of the tree is gold, and the trick is to find its invisible pit: the seed from which new gold may grow. Once discovered, the seed is to be cooked for days and weeks with mercury, sulphur, salt and various inferior metals, until the whole mass suddenly transmutes! So much for the theory. The texts themselves, however, turn out to be just as obscure as they are tantalizing.

"The adept," says the famed *Aurea Catena Homeri*, for example, "should mark well the point that by circulation all things return to the primal matter, or chaotic water." A Chinese recipe adds that "in the sixth month the snow is suddenly seen to fly." By "snow," as it happens, the inscrutable Chinese meant mercury, which their no less inscrutable European colleagues likened to "tiny specks of sun-dust." Raymond Lully, who claimed to have grown gold, said the achievement would be consummated by *"spiritus fugitivos in aere condensatos."*

Typically, these promises ignore the conventional distinctions between the animal, vegetable and mineral kingdoms. They speak instead of energy, flux, and of irreducible entities or what the Greeks called *atomoi*. Thus alchemy brings the wave mechanics, electrons and cloud chambers of modern physics to mind. But the alchemists believed that only a man with golden thoughts and virtues, only a godlike man, could possibly create gold. They thought of laboratory work as an adjunct to spiritual exercise. This kept their science crude, even hopeless in a material sense, although ever young. The Tree of Metals really grew for them. Like daffodils and Easter eggs, or like sugarplums upon a Christmas tree, the golden fruit kept dancing in their heads. Meanwhile it remained out of actual reach.

Yet atomic physics owes a good deal to alchemy's repeated failures. The reason why metals resist transmutation, it now appears, is that most of them are basic elements—as basic, for example, as hydrogen or oxygen. The Tree of Metals holds the very stars in its branches. Can such fundamental stuff ever be cooked up new in a laboratory? Physicists wonder. Some of them are working now on gold.

DEATH AND A PHARAOH

LIKE MELTED CHOCOLATE the Nile flows and fades into the blue Mediterranean. Ascending its indifferent flood through the Delta palms, past loud Cairo and the silent pyramids, past templed Luxor, past the island of Elephantine, southward into Africa a thousand miles and more, one comes at last to Abu Simbel and disembarks. Ramses the Great, Son of the Sun and mightiest of pharaohs, built this place thirty-two centuries since. This was Egypt's southern border. Here Ramses used to sit on state visits, while elephants brought from the wild came trumpeting homage, and giraffes bowed their delicate heads to his knees, and stark-naked Nubian kings presented him with ostrich-feather crowns. It pleased the pharaoh to carve two temples from the cliffs of this burning gate: a modest one for his queen Nefertari and something suitably splendid for himself. His own consisted mainly of not one, not two or three, but four colossal statues of himself, identical, sitting five stories high. The temple interior penetrated past their ankles deep into the cliff. This Ramses adorned with many more statues of himself and painted bas-reliefs of his many battles. Tall and slim as a whirlwind, he still moves along the walls here, effortlessly slaying his enemies. Re-suscitated row on row, they reappear kneeling, elbows tightly bound, adoring him. They lift their heads in ecstasy of torment as like the whirlwind he passes, on he passes: Ramses, forever, into the echoing stone.

Like most pharaohs, Ramses was *café-au-lait* in color, a slender, square-shouldered man with a hooked nose and almond-shaped eyes. His everyday costume was a few yards of semitransparent pleated linen, starched to bell out stiffly from the loins. He also wore pounds of exquisite jewelry, and a wig. Instead of smoking he carried a lotus to sniff, which does seem more dignified. But on ceremonial occasions Ramses put away his lotus and picked up a crook and a flail. In the realm of the dead the god Osiris used these instruments to separate the sheep from the goats. In the realm of the living the god Ramses was supposed to do the same. His hydrant-sized headdress, the red and white "double crown" of upper and lower Egypt, must have given the Pharaoh a head-ache. It was shaped like an enormous bud; a jeweled cobra reared from the brow, and from the chin strap dangled a tuft of human hair. Ramses' mummy and his monuments combine to create a still more specific image: tall and willowy, with very large eyes and a long commanding nose.

Ramses claimed to have commanded an army division in boyhood. He was in his late teens and stood second in line for the throne when his father Seti died. Immediately Ramses killed his older brother and seized full power for himself. Then with characteristic thoroughness he destroyed almost all record of the event and even succeeded in blotting his brother's very name from the pages of history. The country was in a withered mood just then, dreaming of past glories. The temples were crumbling and the frontiers wet with blood. In the north, Egypt's Palestinian empire had fallen away under Hittite influence. In the south, she could barely control the black tribes of Nubia. The "Sand People," or Bedouins, made lightning raids all along the edges of the Nile valley. Worst of all, the wild, axe-wielding Libyans would sometimes appear in the western Delta. Ramses' answer to these afflictions was to stimulate the national economy and bolster Egypt's pride by means of hang-the-cost building and battle. He assembled some twenty thousand warriors, a mighty host for those times, and he larded his force with battle-hardened mercenaries from every corner of the known world. Chief among them were the "Mazoi" of Nubia—ancestors, perhaps, of the lion-hunting Masai in Kenya today. There was also a formidable contingent of yellow-haired, tight-smiling spearmen from "the Islands of the North." These were Greeks, in fact, to whom the distant future belonged. While Ramses mustered his forces, Agamemnon may have been standing before Troy.

Ramses marched and countermarched for two decades. He disciplined the Nubians, chastised the Bedouins, drove off the Libyans. Turning north, he seized the Phoenician capitals, Tyre and Sidon. Then slowly he pushed the Hittites back until at last all of Palestine and Syria were brought under his control. Now Egypt's northern border stood near the high, cold source of the Euphrates. Every autumn Ramses would return triumphantly to Thebes, dragging mile upon mile of chained captives to augment his building program. Among them was the tribe of Israel. It was all due to Ramses' efforts that his descendants could sing:

The princes are prostrate, crying "Mercy!"
Not one raises his head among the Nine Bows.
Desolation is for Tehenu; Hatti is pacified;
Plundered is the Land of Canaan, the evil land;
Carried off is Ascalon; seized upon is Gezer;
Yanoam is done out of existence;
Israel is laid waste, his seed is not;
Palestine is become a widow for Egypt!
All countries together have been pacified.

Ramses fought from a golden chariot. By all accounts a pet lion paced beside him on the bloody field. Strangely reckless, he once battled for two hours before bothering to put on his coat of mail. Another time, near the walls of Kadesh, he fell into a Hittite ambush. Ramses cut his own way out by making six furious sorties in person, with only his honor guard and his lion for company, against thirty-five hundred enemy chariots. This heroic action takes up most of his temple bas-reliefs. Ramses says that in the hour of doom he prayed aloud to his father in faraway Thebes, the sun-god Ammon. The god heard him and strengthened his arm, so that the plain of Kadesh "turned white with corpses." There seems to be no doubt that Ramses in his rage did actually spread panic through the enemy forces, slaughter them in heaps and drive hundreds more to death by drowning in the river that ringed Kadesh. But for all his trying he could not reach the Hittite king Muwatallis, who stood on the far bank of the river, "averted, shrinking, and afraid." After the battle was over, Ramses swore a solemn vow: so long as his span of chariot horses lived on, he would feed them with his own hand.

But like so many epic struggles, the Battle of Kadesh proved indecisive. Ramses never did succeed in humbling the Hittites. At about the age of forty he gave up trying, and concluded a lasting peace. Engraved on silver tablets, the treaty still survives. It calls upon no fewer than four thousand Hittite and Egyptian gods to witness, along with "the sky, the earth, the great sea, the winds and the clouds." Ramses further solemnized the peace by adding a Hittite princess to his already extensive wife collection. Marriage between a pharaoh and a foreigner was unprecedented in Egyptian history. By this intimate gesture Ramses rose above himself to acknowledge the changing world. "He saw that she was fair of face like a goddess," says a temple inscription. "Indeed it was a great, mysterious, marvelous and fortunate affair . . . He loved her more than anything." Marvelous too was the peace and prosperity that came to bless old Egypt for the next half-century. Ramses lived through most of it, on and on, already a legend, his shadow lengthening in sunset. Never again was the land to know such power, wealth or pride as marked his reign.

Ramses ruled, incredibly enough, for sixty-seven years. His old age he devoted to procreation and building. More than a hundred sons were his, and more than a thousand temples and monuments of stone. At Tanis, in the Delta, he constructed a whole new capital, dominated by a statue of himself towering ninety feet into the air. At the base of the statue his subjects would invoke the Son of the Sun with praises such as this:

> *His majesty has built himself a castle, the name of which is "The Great of Victories," and the sun rises and sets within it. Its ships pass and return, so that fresh supplies are there every day, and no lack for anyone. The young men of the Great of Victories are dressed up every day, with sweet oil on their heads, and fresh coiffeurs; they stand beside their doors with their hands full of flowers when Ramses the Great comes by. The ale of the Great of Victories is sweet, and the beer from Cicilia and the wine from the vineyards. And the singers of the Great of Victories are tuneful. So dwell content of heart and free, without stirring hence, O Ramses, thou god!*

Egypt itself was already two thousand years old in Ramses' day. Its history as a nation stretched back to the time when Menes, the first great pharaoh, united the upper Nile and the Delta under one rule. How many nations now boast such antiquity? Yet Ramses never thought of his country as being old at all. He must have considered it eternal, and eternally young. Egypt was the ever-new "gift of the Nile," as Herodotus was to put it. Every year at floodtime the Nile spreads its liquid floor from desert cliffs to desert cliffs, replenishes the life and soil of the valley and flows on, leaving the land spring-green under the brazen sky. As in its soil, so in its kings was the country always renewed. The pharaohs, already comprising nineteen dynasties in Ramses' time, were not regarded as a sequence but rather as a concert of kings: all immortal sons of the same sun-god. Each one dated current history not from some distant past event but from the start of his own reign. The pharaoh's throne seemed the unmoving center of a timeless world. "Once upon a time" meant essentially the same thing as "now."

Ramses' one epithet for non-Egyptians was simply "wretched." To leave their fertile valley, the Egyptians said, meant "going up out of the Black Land" into the "Red Land" of desert, rocks and mountains. True, the foreign gods might succeed in nourishing their Red Land now and again with rain; they even sent rain wastefully down upon the sea. Outlandish gods made other rivers, but the Nile itself was the good serpent and also the backbone of all the earth. Underneath the Nile, they said, flowed another. This Nile traversed a cavern through the whole earth from west to east, crossing below the surface Nile at right angles. And every night the ship of the sun, drawn along by the happy dead, would descend this subterranean Nile eastward to sunrise. Each morning the sun shone again on the invisible crossing of the Niles, while Horus, hawk-god of the horizon, drew his flashing circle round the place. Only here in Egypt were the underworld, the earth and the sky so linked, here at the heart and starting point of all.

Ramses was the personal capstone of the Egyptian pyramid. People must have looked rather like ants or beetles to him, as they do from a skyscraper window. But—his subjects had no elevators by which to reach him. All except a handful remained forever far below. Looking down the slopes of this social pyramid, Ramses would be most conscious of his noble courtiers: good fellows, fond of hunting, feasting, drinking, sex and war. A very few of these favored ones whom he had known since boyhood got to kiss Ramses' slipper now and then instead of the dust before his feet. Next in the social scale came the priests: proud, captious, brilliant, passionately pretending to know more than they did. Ramses steadily enriched them, allowed them to strut all they liked, and meanwhile kept the position of high priest for himself alone. Far down the pyramid, rank on rank, sat his indispensable bureaucracy, the scribes; doubtless a stuffy and rapacious horde. Ramses kept the scribes in line by a rough rule-of-nose: anyone caught with his hand in the till had his nose cut off instanter. Below the scribes came a thin stratum of professionals and private businessmen: the merchants, innkeepers, architects, artists, engineers, musicians, doctors and mummifiers. Then came the soldiers, the sailors and the slaves used for building projects. Finally, at the foot of the pyramid, toiled the land-bound peasants. Nobody knows what their lot was like; they left no records. The artists pictured them as slim, straight and gay, and always at work. Perhaps the peasants lived in a kind of laborious dream, without will, innocent of hope, and neither bad nor good.

Probably everyone except his own valet (a very noble lord) believed that Ramses was a god. Did he himself believe it? What could be more human than to go along with a highly flattering and apparently universal opinion of oneself? Ramses' every word was law, absolute. He had life-and-death mastery over everything in Egypt and in what he knew of Asia and Nubia besides. Moreover, everything and everyone he saw belonged to him personally. He not only ruled his empire; he owned it as well. Think of owning America. Even more, imagine owning practically the whole known world, lock, stock and barrel, yourself! It is all yours, to handle just as you please. Whatever you may choose to do with the world as it rolls along from day to day—things providential, cruel, disastrous or merely whimsical—the people will all bow down and thank you, praising you as a god. All that could turn one's head, maybe. Here is the sort of prayer that the pharaoh, as his own high priest, offered up to his brothers in heaven:

> *And thou shalt give to me health, life, long existence and a prolonged reign; endurance to my every member, sight to my eyes, hearing to my ears, pleasure to my heart, daily. And thou shalt give me to eat until I am satisfied, and thou shalt give me to drink until I am drunk. And thou shalt establish my issue as kings for ever and ever . . .*

Because the Delta is steadily being raised by silt brought down the Nile, its relics of Ramses' reign have long since sunk like reefs below the mud. No one is quite sure where his buried capital of Tanis actually lies. But in the furnace-dry air of the upper Nile, Ramses' stone souvenirs fare relatively well. They are crumbling, to be sure, but imperceptibly. A thirty-three-foot statue of him has been re-erected in Cairo's Station Square. Another even larger portrait still lies where it fell at Memphis. It is superb: elegance writ large, flat on its back. The great temple of Karnak is wide enough to swallow up Saint Peter's and the Vatican together. There Ramses completed the main hall consisting of seventy-three columns, each one as big around as a modern dance floor. The nave is seventy-nine feet high. For himself meanwhile, Ramses constructed a mortuary temple adorned with the single most ambitious work of Egyptian art. This is a tremendous bas-relief showing his victory at Kadesh in full detail. The artists of

Ramses' time had lost the purity and rigor that their ancestors possessed, but he drew overwhelming work from them nonetheless.

A mile or so over the mountains back of his temple lies the barren chasm called the Valley of Kings, a place honeycombed with royal, subterranean, secret tombs. There Ramses had his own final resting place hollowed out and made ready. To preserve the secret of its location, the workmen on the job were slaughtered. He himself was already a living mummy; the tall, willowy body gone wrinkled, frail and sere as ancient parchment. His twelve eldest sons were dead, and still he lived on. Every few years he would celebrate a jubilee, a ritual rejuvenation, and erect a new obelisk in his own honor. Fourteen of these rose at Tanis alone. Rome now has three of his obelisks, and Paris one. Ramses was past ninety in the year 1225 B.C., when death at last came bowing and scraping to summon the sun-god's eldest child down at last from his throne.

One looks back down the deep, deep cavern of the years, into the lost world of Ramses the Great, and sees—what? The glory, the toil, the narrowness, pride and still profundity. Was his an auspicious dawn-hour of the human adventure, or a lurid and ominous sunrise? Absolute despots are notoriously hard to judge. They lack both the rivals and the friends that might provide a sense of scale. Moreover, they have only to dream of glory, and it comes about. On the other hand, it takes a very great man to overcome the negative aspects of those same conditions, to rouse himself and press forward straight to the horizon, to measure himself, since no man else can measure him. This Ramses did. In so doing, he preserved and disseminated a dying culture. For centuries Egypt basked in his afterglow. His legend is undying.

It lives even under other names. The ancient Egyptians made a point of addressing their pharaohs obliquely and obscurely, as a mark of respect. For example, the very word "pharaoh" means simply "palace gate." Among the many names of Ramses himself was *Ozymandias*, a title carved on the pedestal of a huge, ruined portrait in Ramses' mortuary temple at Thebes. This was the inspiration of Shelley's poem:

> *I met a traveller from an antique land,*
> *Who said: Two vast and trunkless legs of stone*
> *Stand in the desert. Near them, on the sand,*
> *Half sunk, a shattered visage lies, whose frown,*
> *And wrinkled lip, and sneer of cold command*
> *Tell that its sculptor well those passions read,*
> *Which yet survive, stamped on these lifeless things,*
> *The hand that mocked them, and the heart that fed:*
> *And on the pedestal these words appear:*
> *"My name is Ozymandias, King of Kings:*
> *Look on my works, ye Mighty, and despair!"*
> *Nothing beside remains. Round the decay*
> *Of that colossal wreck, boundless and bare*
> *The lone and level sands stretch far away.*

Actually, Shelley's own ironic sentiments were not the sort to have been lost on Ramses. Sons of the sun-god expected to be shined upon and wined and dined without stint, but not to live forever here below. Pharaohs might prove startlingly realistic, romantic, and even morbid sometimes. These kings built their tombs and temples of massive stone, in a fantastically successful effort to resist the attrition of millenniums. Everything else they built of brick, and of course it has vanished utterly. Imagine New York City reduced to its churches, monuments and cemeteries alone! Our only clues to ancient Egypt consist in the surviving inscriptions, the art found buried in tomb or temple, and a few tatters from the lost tapestries of Egyptian literature. No doubt these remains are loaded on the side of deathly concerns. Yet there can be no doubt either that it was an old Egyptian custom to dwell on death. The pharaohs and their followers dreaded death, hoped for immortality, and spent a great part of their lives preparing for these things.

One thinks first of the pyramids. Yet nobody knows much about them. Either we have a lot still to learn about the pyramids, or we will never learn it. One of the greatest Egyptologists used to tackle them naked and alone, in the dead of night, with flashlight and tape measure. He had the right idea: combining intense subjective experience with objective measurement. Yet his results were inconclusive. And the tourist fares worse; he fights his way through platoons of idiot dragomen, ducks past camels with names like "Canada Dry," and finally gets inside a dim-lit vein of frighteningly dead air. Imagine Radio City solidified, and without elevators. He climbs and climbs, sweating, to find at last a small office with an empty sarcophagus for a desk. He feels like an applicant too young for the job, faced with the smugness of an executive power which is not only dead, but absent. Having nothing better to do in this granite room, he may pace out a few measurements and even try to calculate the immensities of stone between himself and the sand, himself and fresh air. Like so many others, he counts his steps going down.

This kind of numbers game provides material for quackery; it always has. Yet numerology was ancient (and not exactly primitive) mathematics. And astrology was ancient astronomy. In fact, the priests whom the pharaohs employed had a good deal in common with our own government-supported "exact" scientists. The Egyptian priesthood mastered a good deal of knowledge, especially concerning the night sky. They sought the utmost precision of data and predictability of celestial events. To this end, Egyptian architects provided a marvelous technology. The pyramids square within micromillimeters of "true." What modern building of comparable size does that? The priests drew their knowledge down from the four quarters of heaven, from the sun and moon and planets and innumerable stars, to the exactitude of the pyramids. But that is not all; it seems evident that the pyramids were more than observatories. These geometrical mountains were also intended as royal tombs, and quite possibly as launching pads for pharaonic souls. For example, here is an inscription from an early pyramid, built by a pharaoh named Unis. It would seem to describe him feasting, cannibal-fashion, on the gods themselves:

> *The biggest of them are for his breakfast;*
> *The middle-sized are for his lunch;*
> *Their little ones are for his supper;*
> *Their old folks are for his kindling . . .*
>
> *He has seized the hearts of the gods;*
> *He has eaten the Red;*
> *He has swallowed the Green.*
> *King Unis feeds on contented hearts.*

In Ramses' own day the tombs were different, and so were the incantations. Here is a papyrus from his period which seems to breathe only peace and spiritual joy:

> *Death is before me today*
> *The recovery of a sick man,*
> *Like going out to the garden after sickness.*
>
> *Death is before me today*
> *Like the odor of myrrh,*
> *Like sitting under the sail on a windy day . . .*
>
> *Death is before me today*
> *Like the course of a freshet,*
> *Like coming home from a war-galley.*

The secret tombs in the Valley of Kings, where Ramses had himself laid to rest, were not really tombs at all. Or so the esoteric lore on the subject insists. According to this view, candidates for priesthood used to be drugged and laid out in the so-called tombs. These were chambers carved deep, deep in the living rock, at the ends of sloping and winding tunnels. The interiors were richly adorned with bas-reliefs of the gods in action: cow-headed Hathor, Ibis-headed Thoth, and dog-headed Anubis, Lord of the Dead. Arched across the smooth rock ceiling of the inmost room would be the sky-goddess Nut, the Milky Way, starry comfort for the reawakening initiate, or the dead. If it was really a candidate for priesthood he would light a candle upon awakening, find his way to the tomb entrance, push away the stone there, and reappear, as if newborn to wisdom. This view of things used to find support in the fact that mummies had not been discovered in the cave-tombs. They never were found in the pyramids either. But with the opening of Tutenkhamon's tomb in our own time, the esoteric tradition was badly shaken. When that happened the more orthodox view prevailed. It seemed apparent that Tutenkhamon's tomb had been furnished solely and simply as his own "eternal" abode.

Shortly after "Old King Tut" was buried, at eighteen, grave-robbers made a tentative raid upon him. They were frightened off somehow. For three thousand years the tomb remained undisturbed in the Valley of the Kings, forgotten and lost. The archaeologists who finally happened upon it found a sealed chamber adorned with splendid frescoes and crammed with some of the most luxurious furnishings ever seen on earth. In the center of the chamber stood a golden shrine. Inside the shrine nestled a second one, and inside that a third—all of purest gold. The third shrine held a great sarcophagus cut from a single slab of yellow quartzite, with a rose-granite lid and guardian angels at the four corners. Inside the sarcophagus a gold coffin reposed. The coffin lid was a statue of the boy-king, supine, in gold, with obsidian eyes and a wreath of real flowers at his breast. The flowers had kept their color, by the way. Within this coffin was fitted another, also of solid gold. Inside it lay the royal body, embalmed in pitch and carbonated by internal combustion—like an angry coal.

Ramses' mummy also has come down to us, or rather to the Cairo Museum, but in a less spectacular fashion and by a far less comfortable route. Within a century after his death, a mere moment in Egyptian time, Ramses was robbed blind in his supposedly impregnable tomb by the bold safe-crackers of that age. After the robbers came religious vigilants, a band of pious ghouls. Seeking to protect the still-intact mummy of Ramses, they secretly moved it three times to new hiding places. At last they left it stacked with dozens of other dead pharaohs in an unmarked cave. About a hundred years ago this cave in turn was discovered by robbers, who used it as a combination clubhouse and safe-deposit vault. In 1881 the robbers were caught selling a few remaining trinkets from the mummy-wrappings. Put under torture, they led archaeologists to the spot.

The cult of the dead belongs to Egypt in the same sense that ancestor worship belongs to China, or reincarnation to India. Why should the ancient Egyptians have tried so very hard to prepare for something that is unpredictable and doubtful in every way? Why, again, should their preparations have been so inappropriately physical? Why go to such pains to preserve their own corpses in tombs packed tight with every appurtenance of life on earth? The Egyptians' own banquet songs indicate that they sometimes wondered themselves:

> *Have fun; follow profit;*
> *Fashion your affairs to please yourself.*
> *The day of lamentation comes*
> *When the silent-hearted hears no lamentation.*
> *He that is in the tomb attends not the mourning.*

A coffin used to be produced at the feast to underscore this last message. The concluding verses have an old familiar ring:

Celebrate the glad day!
Go right on rejoicing!
No man takes his own goods with him.
Nobody comes back ever.

They can't use earthly things, and they don't come back; yet perhaps the dead go forward. This last idea keeps reappearing in Egyptian texts. Some tomb inscriptions offer thorough instructions for getting past the judgment seat of Death, for getting out of the underworld courtroom into—? Nothing definite. But all this does militate against the orthodox theory that tombs were "eternal abodes." Somewhere between the seas of terror and the misty cliffs of hope, is there no shoreline, no middle ground?

The ancient Egyptians were apparently terrified not of death itself but of transition to another, unknown world. The problem presented by that one sharp curve up ahead was by far the most important thing in their lives. Imagine yourself awakening from death to an existence utterly strange. Your senses have been stripped away with your flesh. Blind, deaf, weightless, without touch, you hover solitary on the bounds of something, something unimaginable. Compared to this, the pains of death itself were as nothing. This infinitely greater agony, this lingering second death or second birth was what the Egyptians were seeking to live through in their tombs.

That is why a Unis, a Cheops, a Tutenkhamon or a Ramses would spare no effort in preparing for death. That is why they built the tombs that still astonish the world. That, finally, is why they filled their underworlds with pictures and furniture of the most perfect quality—things designed to reassure the soul and ease its still further descent to the Nile of the happy dead: the underground river which becomes the starry sky. Probably the pharaohs' preparations went further still. Having made such enormous efforts to build, secure and properly equip their own tombs, they also occupied them on occasion while still alive! This ghostly ritual provides the missing link between ancient tradition and the evidence of archaeology. It was probably the central rite of the pharaonic "jubilees." Herodotus hints as much in his circumspect conclusion to the story of the Pharaoh Rhampsinitus and the Thief:

And they say that after these things happened the king descended alive into Hades, where he threw dice with the Earth Mother—sometimes winning and sometimes losing. He returned at last to the surface, bearing a golden napkin as a gift from her. They say also that the Egyptians instituted a festival to commemorate Rhampsinitus' descent and return. Now, I myself have seen them celebrating this festival, but I cannot speak with certainty about what lies behind it.

Brave pharaohs such as Ramses practiced death and rebirth, I believe, as one might practice for climbing Mount Everest or diving to the bottom of the ocean. Pity them if you will. Ramses —or "Rhampsinitus," as Herodotus called him—brought back many golden napkins from the underworld. And then finally, no more. But the pains that stretch the spirit cannot be altogether wasted.

THE SEARCH WITHOUT A STOP

I N THE DISTANCE looms a Gothic tower, like an exclamation point overhanging a misty wood. Here at the edge of the wood ripples a lake. An old magician stands upon the shore and lifts a pale sparkling wand. A rowboat glides to the landing. Out of it springs a young hero, all in gold. He rushes upon the magician when—presto—both disappear. But there is a falcon chasing a dove; there is a carp chasing a minnow; there is a fox chasing a hare; there is a speckled chick pecking in the grass. And now the hero, with a haunted look, takes to his boat and pushes off. The magician, breathing hard, doffs the starry cone

142

of his cap and wipes his spangled brow. He grins, bows in our direction, and calls down the mist with his wand.

Vaudeville, was it? Or the secret education of a future king? The magician led the hero on a swift whirl through nature in accustomed forms. To climax the lesson he became a tiny seed, hidden amongst the grass. Thereupon the prince took the shape of a sharp-eyed chick, and swallowed the seed. Not factual knowledge merely but a kernel of human wisdom—something from the sorcerer's own nature—was passed on. The age-old show stands for historic actuality: teaching as it has been and ought still to be practiced.

When studies are kept personal and various, they make for great expectations and modesty combined. They prepare the ground for genius in a few, and they deepen the sense of search in all. What if we do seem like foolish chickens scratching for seeds before the gates of paradox? Those seeds are spirit-gold, nourishment forever. "We each must eat our peck of dust," or must we? Robert Frost, feeling good, once crowed:

> *Such was life in the Golden Gate;*
> *Gold dusted all we drank and ate,*
> *And I was one of the children told,*
> *"We all must eat our peck of gold."*

However, we stick mainly to the dust method. Competition, specialization and a great dearth of ordinary give and take combine to smother what the student might have been. Home comes the brittle product we know so well: the Mandarin. He's everywhere now. The Mandarin proves useful enough in technology (whatever his particular field may be) but how useful is he to himself? That is another question. He will be pitied, of course. Efforts will be made to console him for he knows not what.

They say religion is a great consolation to most. But the story behind the statistics is peculiar. Until recently, religious people believed that their particular ministers of God conversed with God. How many really believe it now? Remove that belief and religion becomes a question of sentiment, or search again. Not very consoling, in either case. More consoling, for millions of good folk today, are the gleaming new station wagons in which they drive to church. Or perhaps the Rome vacation which includes a papal audience and a dinner at Alfredo alla Scrofa's. Or, for the economy-minded, a Sunday ballgame on TV. Or maybe just a phone call to a friend, praying he'll be there. If he's not, put on another record, or take an aspirin. In our time technology, and not religion, is really the "opiate of the people."

Just as surely as puritan religion ruled the pilgrim fathers of America, technological orgy and glut command us now. Moreover the cold comforts of technology can be ruinous, objectively and subjectively as well. To destroy the wilderness, to raise our kids on ever more powerful pills and nastier hypodermics, to force up enormous and unwanted single crops with chemicals, to pollute our streams and lakes and swim in chlorine, to set the air about our ears ajolt with jets, to shower soot and cinders on ourselves, to strip our hills of trees, to create vast dumping-grounds of radioactive waste, to pile horrid cities ever higher in eye-smarting and lung-hurting smog—at least some of these things are ugly, no? But there is something uglier still in us, some urge to demean the delightful mother of us all. She groans and sickens now beneath our nerveless whips. By brutally extorting nature's gifts—as if that were the only way to have them—we orphan man.

Suicidal lordliness is nothing new of course. What is new is the technology to make it stick. By way of contrast, consider Herodotus' historical account of proud king Xerxes and the Hellespont. When he first tried to cross this turbulent strait, the stream rose and carried off Xerxes' bridges. Thereupon he had it symbolically fettered, branded and given three hundred splashing lashes. Meanwhile his ministers hectored the hurrying waters in no uncertain terms: "Oh, salt and bitter stream, your master lays this punishment upon you . . . He intends to cross you anyhow . . . Nobody sacrifices to you, for you deserve neglect!" Herodotus concludes this quotation with a stern appraisal. He calls it "a highly presumptuous way of addressing the Hellespont, and typical of a barbarous nation."

All nations are ten times as barbarous now. Who so much as bothers to spit in a river today, let alone greet it, even with a curse? We begin to think that nature is not there, except for human convenience. And heaven really does arm with pride those whom it wishes to destroy.

Where wast thou when I laid the foundations of the earth? So Jehovah demanded, out of the whirlwind. Where indeed? *When the morning stars sang together, and all the sons of God shouted for joy?* Job was overawed by the question, as everybody knows. He repented in dust and ashes. Yet the question remains; insistent, liberating. *Where wast thou?* And something inside a man leaps up to answer: "I was there, for I too have been a son of heaven!" But then he recollects himself; his heart sinks, perhaps he "repents." Still the question remains. The whirlwind returns.

A man cries out in his sleep. Coming awake, he feels along the bedside table for his cigarettes, lights one, and goes to the window. He had been wrestling with an angel . . . or a monster. He exhales, blurring the stars.

The night sky is a paradoxical tapestry, woven of unknown airs and fires, unknown attractions, distances, velocities. The dark mountain before him is equally mysterious; an immense heaping of minerals and springs, home to a host of wild things. He feels so ignorant, not as a child but only as a grown person can. The sense of search yearns and stirs and cries out in his blood. He longs to see the universe complete, to penetrate or turn it while he can, to know just how it works out there. And inside himself as well. For in dreams he has been treading the enormous night. The universe is inside also.

Never will science satisfy the sense of search. A science which even pretends to turn the tapestry of night has ceased to be science and become dogma. Nor will dogma satisfy the sense of search; for how can we firmly believe what is unknown? Yet scientists and dogmatists of all descriptions crowd into the mind of the man at the window: grimacing, clamoring, howling their separate invitations and insane rebukes.

What is it that he really seeks? Is it forgetfulness, perhaps? Or knowledge, and the power that comes with knowing? Some psychologists go so far as to say that the sense of search is really sexual! The man at the window flicks his cigarette away, into the darkness. Who would question the need to learn things and forget them again? Who dares to swim against the swift rip tides of sex? And who can deny the fact of some still stronger pull? Something impersonal, unbidden, vast, unceasing? As the sun works upon the plants, drawing them up out of themselves, so this force works upon the minds of men.

A mother eagle turns her chicks to face the sun. Those who blink or turn away, she deliberately starves. Such is the legend, anyhow. It has been told wherever eagles or their like played a part in the lives of men. The Plains Indians of North America believed it. The braves adorned themselves with eagle feathers, and like the eagle they too worshiped the sun. Every midsummer they did marvelous and painful homage to the sun. This was a prehistoric rite, but the Indians' stone age briefly interpenetrated civilization. And so we have actual records of the Gazing at the Sun Dance, as the Oglala Sioux performed it.

At the burning center of the year, upon the open plain, the entire tribe convened. Their preparations for the dance took seven days. First a straight-growing poplar tree was felled and smoothed. The braves brought it into camp and striped it lengthwise with red, blue, green and yellow, to represent the four quarters of the world. Then they cut out a section of turf, about twenty feet square, to make a dancing place. They raised an earth altar at the center, topped with a layer of crimson clay which was quartered by a glittering mica cross. They stood their striped pole in a pit which struck down through the altar. Two lumpish effigies dangled from the pole; a man and a buffalo of painted hide. Now the stage was set; everyone assembled, and the medicine men sang out:

> *At the center of the Earth*
> *Stand looking around you!*
> *Recognizing the tribe*
> *Stand looking around you!*

Carnival followed: loud, licentious, orgiastic, into the night. With sunrise, the climax approached. A band of painted warriors roughly restored order. Their winged arrows cut down the effigies from the pole. Now a dozen or more young braves—volunteers—gathered at the altar. They wore otter-skin aprons only. Whistles made of eagle bones were between their teeth. Their hands and feet were painted red. Suddenly, older warriors pounced upon the motionless volunteers, flung them to the ground and bound them fast. Then with stone knives they slit open the flesh of the dancers' chests, shoulders and backs. They pushed wooden pegs through the muscles, between the slits of skin. They tied rawhide cords to the pegs. Some of these cords were made fast to the pole, and others to buffalo skulls lying loose. Then the torturers stood back; the drumming and the singing began; the sun rose higher; the prisoners began to dance. They danced, and danced in agony, gazing at the sun, blowing their eagle whistles, adoring, hour by hour. Sometimes they rested briefly, while sworn maidens would step forward to wipe the blood from their wounds. Then the drumming, singing and dancing would begin again. The midsummer sun stood blazing now, straight overhead. There was no shade at all, only the jiggling shadows of the thongs. Now, at a signal from the medicine men, the drumming grew yet more intense; the dancers were to be allowed a wilder dancing; now they were to tear their own flesh loose, if they could, from the piercing pegs. Thus they found release as the chanting rolled to a peak of ecstasy, welcoming the new-fledged eagles—Sons of the Sun.

Barbarous? And yet behind the torment lay religious longing of a generous kind. A Sioux medicine man explained the point of the rite this way: "We know that all the creatures on the earth were placed here by Wakantaka. So if a man says he will offer up a horse, he is only giving what belongs to Wakantaka already. I might offer tobacco or other valuables, but if I kept back the rest, who would believe I was in earnest? So I promise to give my own body." It was understood that before the end of summer each dancer would receive a dream-visit from his heavenly father. Somehow, this promise also was fulfilled. It is a matter of record that those who danced the sun-dance kept a certain cheerful dignity throughout their lives. The searching fires of their father the sun had pierced the very marrows of their bones: they were tempered.

From stone age to atomic age to . . . the suffering and joy, the searching and the tempering continue. The sun dust swirls. Because we are suffering and joy in ourselves, we are searching and tempering in ourselves. Also, it seems that we are sun dust. At the California Institute of Technology, physicists guess that all the elements evolved from a primal cloud of hydrogen, cooked in the bellies of forefathering stars.

Scientists are drawing intensely violent and romantic pictures of late. They say that our moon is a whitecap torn from the Pacific Ocean's tallest tidal wave. When Earth still spun molten through the vast, its tides were liquid basalt and its spume glowing granite, until at last the moon emerged from the mineral sea. Cooling as she sailed and hardening as she cooled, the moon made a bright fist, and drawing her invisible reins about the Earth, she steadied us. The stone tides fell. The dark sharp breath of space cooled our scarred globe. Hissing oceans and skies of thick rolling steam surrounded us. Meanwhile lightning fingered the thick wet hair of the world, shaking it mightily. There was no oxygen as yet, nor even a molecule of organic life.

At the University of Chicago, a test run of such conditions has been made. Chemists mingled hydrogen, methane and ammonia with double-distilled water, and passed this lethal concoction through a powerful electric field, day after day. To their amazement, carbon molecules finally formed in the tormented stream. Since these are the "building blocks of life," it seems that lightning made life possible. Like so many scientific discoveries, this one seems to echo a heart-knowledge which has been manifested many times over in the myths of man. Here for instance is a practically forgotten Orphic legend about the lightnings of the greatest Greek deity:

In the beginning, Father Zeus and his family of gods ruled the sky alone. Titans occupied the earth, and there were no people. As time went by the titans conceived an envious hatred for the youngest son of Zeus: a golden-haired god-child. With tops of different sorts, and jointed dolls, and apples from the clear-voiced Hesperides, they beguiled him down into their dark forest. Once the titans had the child in their secret power, they slew him, dismembered him, and boiled his remains in a cauldron. Greedily, they devoured every scrap. They were hoping thus to partake of the child's immortality. Meanwhile Zeus was wandering, disconsolate, in search of his son. He soon found the flesh-stuffed feasters. He saw from their shining eyes what they had done. A Homeric hymn (translated by Jack Lindsay) tells of the god's anger:

Then Zeus no longer held back his power. On the height
his heart was swarming with fury, and all his might
he uttered forth. From Heaven and Olympus he swung,
tossing his lightning-darts. The bolts he flung
were fierce with thunder and lightning, and thickly they came
out of his strong right hand with a sacred flame
rolling: the life-giving earth with a shudder of sound
took fire, and measureless forest crackled around.
All land was seething and heaving, and Ocean-stream
and the barren sea. Lapped round with a fiery steam
stood the earthborn Titans. Numberless flames were blown
to the brightening aether. Glare of the thunder-stone
and lightning blinded the eyes of the strongest there.

The titans were almost all burnt up. But from their ashes, mankind came into being. Each man a prey to the sins of giants, filled with guilts and fears, and yet flickeringly godlike too. Since each man contains a dark sparkling cinder of the son of heaven, immortal. We still say, "ashes to ashes, dust to dust." And we still have intimations of immortality.

The Greek poet Epimenides wrote that in Zeus "we live and move and have our being." Cleanthes described all mankind as "the children of Zeus." So the Greeks were prepared to accept the monotheism of Saint Paul. However, they still had room in their hearts for a host of lesser gods: Poseidon, Aphrodite, Ares and the rest. All of whom together personified the forces which hold the world in balance. God *and* nature ruled.

It was a dark day when the church fathers decided to make demons of the pagan gods. What followed was a slow, forced separation of Christian thought from nature—and from natural passions. Few modern scientists make much point of being Christians, granted. Yet their coldly analytical attitude to nature, and to human nature, stems from the early Christian struggle against pagan worship.

Take Poseidon, of the shaggy dark-blue hair. He it was who kept Odysseus from sailing straight home after the sack of Troy. Was this a willful or a righteous act? Neither precisely, since Poseidon in this case means the changeable sea, which he ruled. Or take Ares, the straight-limbed god of war. In a sense he actually was war. So the famous epitaph of Timokritos was not meant to malign Ares; it stated what used to be a fact of battle:

> *Timokritos fought well. This is his grave.*
> *For Ares spares the coward; not the brave.*

And then, Aphrodite. Of all the Greek pantheon, she is the most sorely missed today. People who mistake sex for a thing of sordid pleasure, guilt and shame, are furthest away from the goddess. Foam-born Aphrodite can't be bought, not for love or money. Nor is she ever—in herself—a cause for regret. She comes as a gift and goes again, like a fair wind off the sea. Yet she was not only an immensely powerful divinity, but also the very act of love. And that is why not even the immortals—except virgin ones—escaped her rule.

On the Aegean island of Lemnos was a fire lit by no human hand. The flame sprang up from the mothering earth of its own will, blazing intermittently. We would call it a seepage of natural gas with a low flash point. The Greeks called it Hephaistos: god of technology and art. He was a "wind-child," born to Hera with no help at all from her husband. Devotees of the fatherless god used to watch his wind-bent flames melting and fusing the ores of the surrounding cliffs. This taught them the beginnings of a very forceful magic: metallurgy. Hephaistos it was who fashioned the great shield of Achilles, so lovely in detail, so awesome in the round. Achilles' shield, said Homer, "flashed in the distance like the full moon, or like the gleam from a bonfire on a lonely upland farm, which sailors barely glimpse as they are driven away down the highways of the fish by offshore gales."

Achilles' armor felt light as a pair of wings. It lifted up the hero's heart and readied him to slay. He knew that he would kill Hector, and be killed soon afterwards. The thread of his own fate was twisted together with his enemy's. Yet he rushed fiercely to meet his doom; not because the gods insisted on it but because the poets expected nothing less. He would give his last breath to glory; glory drew him on. Achilles armed has been compared to a glistening tornado of fine bright needles, all magnetized by glory.

That is by the way. What drew the god Hephaistos himself was love-making. At first he claimed Athena, the virgin goddess of wisdom, for his muse. He took her by surprise one day and tumbled her, thrusting his fire between her snowy thighs. Smiling, the Maiden pushed him off; his seed fell upon the ground. From this frustrating encounter sprang the first of the race of statues; sculpture came to be.

After this, Hephaistos actually married Aphrodite. It seems that he expected the goddess of love to reduce her domain to himself. Might as well attempt to squeeze the universe into a ball. Not even wild beasts may flee the goddess or avoid her glance. Aphrodite goes wherever the soft winds blow. Hephaistos could sooner have tied a cloud to his bedpost. Well, jealousy will try anything, and succeed in nothing. Except murder sometimes; but there is no way of murdering an immortal. Hephaistos thought to punish his bride with shame. Sweating at his forge, the artful deity hammered out an unbreakable and almost invisible net of bronze meshes. This he concealed above his nuptial couch. Aphrodite was having an affair with Ares. The next time they frolicked, down came the net. Hephaistos, rushing in, loudly called upon the gods to witness fair Love and War, caught fast. The gods gathered at once, and each of them wished to trade places with poor scowling Ares! Aphrodite, bathed in their desiring glances, laughed for sheer pleasure; her glistening prison trembled. Answering laughter, unquenchable, arose among the immortals. Hephaistos seemed the only miserable person present; rightly so. There was nothing for it but to free his catch.

The delights of love are too precious to police, too funny to frown upon, and too good to miss. Such are the obvious morals of this rather risqué tale. One might add that every animal knows how to love, but the gods can laugh about it.

Of course, this kind of myth has been troubling to scholars. Most especially to those who were brought up in a churchly tradition. Such men will boggle and hedge to mitigate the good Greek earthiness. For instance, the esteemed Gilbert Murray cautioned colleagues to "remember that these gods are not real people with a real character . . . They change every time they are thought of, as a word changes every time it is pronounced." True, but don't we all?

On a more abstract level, Hephaistos stands for technology itself. Then Aphrodite becomes the free abundance of nature—and Ares uncaring war—meanly trapped together in a metal net. The parallel with modern times is almost too painful to pursue. But the Greek deity released his captives; what will ours do? Laughter persuaded Hephaistos to relent. Imagine the masters of our own destinies paying heed to laughter! Now the whole world huddles in a technological web, and the Lords of the Web are humorless. Worse, they are fanatics, by and large. They have no peace; how could they let go?

In India the favorite name for a girl is Shantih—Peace. And yet, as an Indian statesman has confessed, "There is no *shantih* in all India." No inward peace. Nowhere is there such a thing any more perhaps. Not in any single area. Only in some hearts, scattered. Where one does come across it in an individual, does one also find a jellyfish personality? Does peacefulness make a man spineless? Fanatics assume so, that much is true. But the person with *shantih*, with peace in his heart, is really formidable. In the good sense, since he has self-sufficiency besides. This is the spontaneous man, not easy to find.

Fanatics actually shape us most of the time. We go on thinking thoughts of a fanatic strain; thoughts that are really too stiff and cold for minds at body temperature. Also, we spend our days performing tasks unsuited to our natural powers. This is not to blame the present age; we can't change it anyhow. Only ourselves.

A fanatic is a white knight on a hobbyhorse who thinks his armor doesn't squeak. He rides everywhere, including a lot of places where horses are not meant to go. He dismounts with difficulty, if at all. Nothing for himself does he ask, but only sugar for his horse. His horse never eats people, he'll remark: "It's the kingliest and kindest of beasts, expressly created to help humanity." And he flashes a shining white-knight smile, sincerely meant to reassure. What, still no sugar? Then comes a change of tone: "My horse is large, very large. Observe its flowing mane, its flaming eye. Can't you recognize the brute power I have reined in here under me? Give sugar!" And if he does have power, better give. But in a free society this need not be. Perhaps in certain company his hobbyhorse looms small indeed? Then of necessity the fanatic takes still another tone: patience. Deliberately enunciating each word syllable by separate syllable as in the well-known "Chinese water torture" he produces one hundred and one apt quotations on the merits of a steed like his. Still not impressed? Then you're a fool, or what is worse a dilettante, badly in need of instruction. So he lifts and counts up for you hair by hair each and every hair of his nag's tail. Hah! Thought he couldn't do it, eh? You stifle a yawn; he mistakes this for a sneer—and burns to ride you down. He's starving, poor knight. Just a hollow reed in all that hollow armor. And there's nothing whatsoever to be done about it.

It might be argued that the Sioux Indian sun-dancers, the Orphic poets and perhaps the physicists have been fanatics too. No doubt some have been. However, a distinction ought to be made between the man who starves because his heart is empty, and the man who starves because his heart is full.

The king who toppled Troy wore a mask of beaten gold in his tomb. I think this was in hopes that his father, the sun-god, would recognize the filial glint of it. The golden eyes were squinted shut, perhaps as a protection against the god's welcoming radiance. There were golden flowers also at his side, and golden butterflies, and tiny golden weighing scales. Exquisite things, miniaturized, furniture for an ethereal voyage. Agamemnon's tomb at Mycenae is enormous, beehive shaped, smooth within, a hollow hill. Such were the mausoleums of Cyclopean lords. One finds them as far west as Spain. And later peoples, coming upon these tombs, mistook them for caves of love. They thought that olden giants, living in the open, had hollowed out the underground domes for private amours. Appropriately enough, archetypal lovers of medieval legend retired to just such a cave. Gottfried von Strassburg's *Tristan and Isolde* describes it (in A. T. Hatto's fine translation):

> *This grotto was round, broad, high, and perpendicular, snow-white, smooth, and even, throughout its whole circumference. Above, its vault was finely keyed, and on the keystone there was a crown most beautifully adorned with goldsmiths' work and encrusted with precious stones. Below, the pavement was of smooth, rich, shining marble, as green as grass. At the center there was a bed most perfectly cut from a slab of crystal . . . In the upper part of the grotto some small windows had been hewn out to let in the light, and these shone in several places . . . At their due times you could hear the sweet singing of the birds. Their*

music was so lovely—even lovelier here than elsewhere. Both eye and ear found their pasture and delight here: the eye its pasture, the ear its delight. There were shade and sunshine, air and breezes, both soft and gentle . . . Man was there with Woman, Woman there with Man. What else should they be needing? They had what they were meant to have; they had reached the goal of their desire.

But—what did they have to eat? The chronicler answers firmly: "There is enough here in my opinion. If anyone has discovered better nourishment in this world, let him speak in the light of his experience. There was a time when I, too, led such a life, and I thought it quite sufficient."

Tristan and Isolde joyfully starved in their tomb of love, because their hearts were full. In love, in one another, they had found personal answers to ultimate questions. Yet at last they left the Cave for the Court, and tragedy. Not even love can satisfy the sense of search.

Personal answers to ultimate questions. These are just what we seek. All of us, in company at first, in love if we be fortunate, and then at last alone. At last the search itself gives answer, and the answer is a life. Once long ago a Greek poet named Empedocles wrote a personal homage to the elements. It has been lost, but the legend of his passionate searching has not been lost. Empedocles drew nature to his heart. He even drank fire—once. They found his sandals on Mount Etna in Sicily, at the brink of the volcano. No doubt he had slipped them off instinctively, like a swimmer, before immolating himself. Empedocles flung back his bones down dark stairwells of bubbling stone, to the beginnings of the world. But his sandals betrayed him. It seems the poet meant to vanish without a trace, as if he had never died.

Sixty miles underneath us molten rock begins, elastic as a red rubber ball. The continents, pressed down during the last ice age, are rising again now. Such is the more or less true mythology taught in our schools. Latin schoolboys heard a different story. Far beneath Mount Etna moved a god, Vulcan, furiously forging thunderbolts. Hairy, forge-blackened, crude, Vulcan was a western cousin to Hephaistos. One-eyed Cyclopes danced attendance on him. Vulcan's two subsidiary workshops, Stromboli and Vesuvius, were connected with Etna underground. Sicilians, Strombolians, Neapolitans and Pompeians all lived in dread of his rage. His very sweat boiled. Vulcan would swallow mossy boulders, like grapes, to quench his thirst. At night his lovesick roars burst open cavern walls. Hopeful worshipers said he really had a good mate, and that her name was *Mater Stabilis*—"Steady Mother."

As further insurance, Italians regaled him with good sea food, typically enough. Under Vesuvius, at evening by the darkening blue bay, they would build golden bonfires and immolate choice fish in Vulcan's name. While eagles glinted in the last rays of sunset far above, soaring higher to say goodnight.

Six centuries and more before the birth of Christ, a bearded prophet stood on a mountain in the east of Persia, gazing into the heavens. It is related that "a stream from a star" descended upon him, setting the whole peak afire. Yet he returned unscathed to his valley. Thereafter this man preached the worship of one god only, Ahuramazda, lord of all the fires of heaven. The prophet himself took the ancient name Zarathustra, which means "Living Star." People asked what sacrifices ought to be made, honoring the god of light. And he replied: "As an offering, Zarathustra brings the life of his own body." Then he lit a wood fire upon a pure altar under the open sky. Zarathustra himself guarded and carefully tended his little blaze. Until one day a band of unbelievers came and cut the prophet's throat at his altar, drowning the flame in blood.

At about the same moment in history, an Ionian scientist named Heraclitus sat gazing into his hearth. He saw leaping and sparkling there a sure defense against savage beasts, against cold, and the illimitable dark. Also he saw man's chief agent for manipulating things: the mighty spirit of the forge. And something more, thought Heraclitus, something more. The flames were dancing in his head now, crackling as if to speak. Where lies God's hearth? At the sun, perhaps. And whereby does God shape nature? Heraclitus brooded on this question until his fire slept, and he too dreamed. The next day he announced a new belief: All the world is fire-formed and lives by the interior touch of flame. The whole world is a waterfall of fire and also a fountain of sparks. All matter lives. A person's own body is a burning house. So, more slowly burning, is a snow-capped peak, a mountain close to the fires of the stars.

Heraclitus had no way of proving his ideas by experiment, and they were soon supplanted. Yet Plato was to follow Heraclitus' lead in picturing fire as a vital entity. He said it swarmed with pyramid-shaped atoms. These, jiggling together, "produce a fine-chopping effect which we feel as heat." Intuition told Plato that heat is really a form of motion. He failed to take the matter just one step further and eliminate "fire atoms" entirely. Fire seems not to need a body of its own; it dies and is reborn in everything —or almost everything. Astrophysicists argue that our sun is "too hot" to burn. It just shines: *Let there be light!*

Venerable Heraclitus returns to favor. Science again reveals that fire is the world's heart and also the life of this planet Earth, poured from without. Plants accumulate sunlight in the form of sugars, by a process known as "photosynthesis." (This has been approximated in a laboratory.) Green plants use some sugars to grow on, while producing an enormous surplus. All organic life on Earth, without exception, draws directly or else indirectly from this. Living energies are oxidation—the burning—of crystalized sunlight. Earth is on a green-gold standard, set by the sun. Life is one fire, strictly so.

All things are fed on fire and feed the fire. Who knows if it will ever cease?

PART FOUR

WATER

Sunset off Cape Sounion: from the temple dedicated to Poseidon, Earth-Shaker, he of the shaggy dark-blue hair.

On the island of Elephantine: a fish carved in the cliff seems like water brought to life, a spontaneous child of the Nile.

RIVER WRESTLER

IN THE ANCIENT Greek city of Thebes there stands a well-wrought palace, and in that palace there is a courtyard with a cool and musical fountain. A low door leads from the courtyard into a darkened nursery. A baby boy sleeps there, rosy in his cradle, dreaming that he is a god. While two enormous snakes come swelling out of the fountain, gliding across the cold flagstones of the courtyard, smoothly, silently sliding into the nursery, to the cradle. They rear their scaly heads at the baby; their jaws are parting; they show their frothing fangs; their forked, crimson tongues are flicking about his ears. The baby

163

awakens, smiling. He does not cry out when he sees the snakes. Instead he sits up in his cradle and resolutely takes their necks in his chubby hands.

He was born to destroy the beasts of our fear. He strangled the serpents, they say. And yet this grim scene, so often represented in classical art, may have been misinterpreted. Possibly the snakes came to purify the baby's hearing with their fiery tongues, in order that he might listen to heaven, all his days. The Greek ideal in war and athletics was "making the hands keep the head." Meaning: to defend oneself at all times. In domestic life the Greeks reversed the ideal. There they favored "making the head keep the hands." Meaning: don't grab. And if it be true that the serpents came to endow the baby with the gift of prophecy, then it must also be true that he drew these hissing benefactors ever so gently to himself.

Why are streams greater than brooks, rivers greater than streams, and seas greater than rivers? Obviously, because they are lower down. There is something about water which teaches humility, not of a mawkish but of a spontaneous kind. Nothing on earth is more powerful—or more serviceable—than water. It takes whatever comes, and it reshapes everything. The boy in the cradle grew up to be like that. He would wrestle with rivers, yet he was like a river himself. His very name, which the Oracle of Delphi gave to him, had a paradoxically majestic modesty about it. The Romans called him "Hercules," as most people still do. But his Greek name was Heracles. And the *Hera* stood not for the goddess Hera (as is often supposed) but for "service." While *cles* meant "renown."

All that we know of Heracles comes from ancient art, and from legend—which is the same thing as saying semifiction. In his case the legends are drawn from a deep well indeed, from long before Homer, and before Greek history itself began. Therefore they are often self-contradictory, and open to various interpretations. The Greek playwrights made him passion's plaything.

The stoic philosophers, on the contrary, thought him a stoic. Astrologists read his labors as a progress through the signs of the zodiac. A student of Sir James Frazer's *Golden Bough*, or of Robert Graves, may call Heracles a figure of bloody superstition. Such modern scholars as Kerenyi and Fontenrose see him as a champion against "Death." But looking at the whole of Heracles' story one cannot help noticing how it will dwarf any one man's view. For if the literature in itself is vast, Heracles' behind-the-scenes influence on human thought and action has been incalculably great. Detailed scholarship collapses, like a pup tent in a gale, before this benevolent thunderhead. No mere examination of the evidence, however elaborate, can put him in perspective. Heracles will never be anatomized. Instead, he has to be imagined.

For many people, Glycon's statue of him is what springs first to mind. This monstrous, marble-muscled weight-lifter, pin-headed, glooms in the Naples Museum, leaning upon an enormous club. It is a beached whale of gym or stadium or wrestling ring. Nobody so belted and hung about with muscles could have had the speed or grace to do more than a tenth of what Heracles accomplished. Glycon tried to create the figure of a single man having the strength of ten men. But the all-round athlete is not like that; he simply makes the right move at the right moment. Against Glycon's image ought to be set an archaic head of Heracles in the Agora Museum at Athens. This fist-size fragment, one of the most marvelous relics of the sixth century before Christ, is clear-browed, wide-eyed, lean of cheek, and firmly smiling. It chimes well with Euripides' one-line description of the hero: "Straightforward, unadorned; at his best in crises."

His first chance to serve mankind as a water-tamer came soon after leaving Delphi, when he arrived at the seaside town of Lerna. The people on the street were silent, pale and apparently consumed with fear. Why? Heracles, burning with curiosity and the hope of adventure, pulled up at a tavern in the center of town.

He ordered beef and wine for himself and his charioteer; then, while eating, he questioned the proprietor. It seemed that the whole village was mortgaged to a terrible monster called Hydra. The name related to water, but Hydra was no ordinary spring. She lived beneath a plane tree further on, where the road dipped towards the beach. Her seven venomous serpent heads would often burst from the ground together and spill flickering across the way into the sea. She was a fountain of evil, taking toll of travelers. The young gentlemen had better avoid her, the proprietor concluded, and go back the same way they had come. Heracles thanked him and went on eating. His club, a little over three feet long, of knobby, polished olive wood, leaned against the table at his side. When he had done, he rose, brushed himself off, took up his club, nodded to his charioteer, and ducked silently out the door. The townspeople, peering through their bolted shutters, saw him stroll to the plane tree and stand in its shade, idly twirling his club in one hand. He was whistling, as if to himself, but Hydra heard him and she boiled blackly up.

Instantly he waded in against her, with his club flashing, bashing and thudding amongst the liquid, lethal heads that spread twining, surrounding, filling the dappled shade with poison froth. Soon Heracles was in serious trouble. For each darting, mucky head that he crushed, two new ones instantly grew. And as if that were not enough a giant crab sidled up out of the sea behind him as he fought, pincering Heracles' ribs in the barnacled vise of a gate-sized claw. It was then that Heracles' charioteer, waiting under orders at the tavern, heard a shout that would never once be heard again: his master's cry for help in battle. The youth snatched a burning branch from the tavern hearth, dashed to the rescue, and drove his weapon's fiery point against the eyes of the implacable crab. The murderous claw fell open; Heracles bounded free. As silently as it had come, the crab retreated wincing underneath the waves.

When evening fell upon the blood-soaked shore, Hydra lay

hissing and frothing still—but she also had gone down in defeat, safely pinned and imprisoned "beneath a stone." What sort of stone? Who knows? They say that it was very large, and that is all. But there is one interesting clue: Lerna, the site of the struggle, changed its name to Miloi, which is Greek for "the Mills," and Miloi it remains today. This suggests that Heracles succeeded in confining the raging waters to a single channel and that he, so to speak, squeezed Hydra into a millrace. In which case the mysterious stone above the deathless monster's prison must have been and must still remain a millstone, forever grinding as she groans to make man's bread.

It must be confessed that before leaving Hydra to her new career of service Heracles knelt down and delicately dipped his stock of arrows into her—to poison them. Although he was to prove himself as generous-hearted as any man in history, he was obviously no saint.

The age of Heracles was very like our own wild West only wilder; with no sheriffs and no schoolteachers, pretty or otherwise. Cattle country then included all of southern Europe and most of the Middle East besides. Throughout this vast territory, cattle were the normal medium of exchange, borderlines were fluid, and hostile tribes battled for pasturage or for their ancient hunting grounds. Killing, burning, lynching, raping, raiding and rustling were the order of the day. Cattle barons passed for kings, and any horseman was a noble. Crooks were crooks, of course, and they were everywhere. Herocs were comparatively few in number, then as now. Heroes need elbow room.

Heracles violently obeyed the not-so-golden rule of his time: "Do unto others as they would like to do unto you." Consider for example his handling of King Diomedes. This ruler was lavishly hospitable, but easily bored. Whenever a guest offended or began to pall, Diomedes would take the man out back and feed him to the horses. In fact, he kept a stableful of man-eating mares for just that purpose. To stop the practice, Heracles now traveled on from Lerna to Diomedes' county. It was evening when he topped a rise of land and saw the palace half a mile ahead, all atwinkle with welcoming torches. Heracles said goodbye to his brave charioteer and strolled on alone through the gathering gloom. Soon afterwards he was shaking the gates, roaring for admission. Diomedes, who was at dinner, smiled, licked his fingertips and ordered that the loud stranger be welcomed at once to the feast. Within the next few hours Heracles ate and drank far more than was proper, boasted some, sang a couple of bawdy songs and—went to sleep where he sat. Diomedes, beaming now, detailed six of his strongest men to carry Heracles up to the main guestroom. It looked as if this large buffoon would give the horses something to chew on for quite a while. But he wanted the man conscious.

At about the witching hour Heracles awakened, much refreshed. He slipped downstairs to finish off the wine jar in the dark, yawned, and made his leisurely way out to the stable. The mares whinnied hungrily. Stepping light and fast now, he opened their stall and swung up onto the leader's back. As she reared, he kicked his heels hard against her ribs, twined a hank of her mane in his fist and brought her out from the barn at a gallop. The others followed, snorting, manes tossing silver in the moonlight, through the yard, over the fence and away for the starry horizon before the guards could so much as draw breath to cry, "Thief!"

By dawn Heracles had reached the shore, and his mares were played out. He galloped them across a tidal basin which happened to be dry at that hour, and tethered them on a sandbar some distance from shore. The pearly light turned pink as the sun rose; ruby rivulets meandered towards shore. Meanwhile, as Heracles had expected, a cavalry pursuit led by Diomedes appeared and made straight for him over the shell-strewn basin of sand. But Heracles ignored them; he had found an old timber from a wreck and he was using it to dig a channel through the sandbar, really putting his back into the work, lost from sight within a purple cloud of flying sand. Now the sea started thrusting through the channel, its mounting rush shouldering even Heracles to one side. He scrambled for the bank and stood still, shading his eyes to see his pursuers tumbled and drowned amid the oncoming waves. There was only one man whom he cared to rescue: Diomedes. After some time Heracles waded out to collar the king, dragged him from the brine and flung him as a breakfast to the ravening mares. It seemed to quiet them.

Cruel Diomedes had been brought low without recourse to weapons, only with water. The Red Sea drowning of Pharaoh's forces, when they pursued Moses, is an obvious parallel. But what happened to the man-eating mares? As former instruments of human sacrifice, they were sacred and inviolable. So Heracles herded them to a mountain fastness, empty of mankind, where they learned to like grass.

On his way back from the wilderness, Heracles fell into ambush. Minyan savages trapped him in a thicket for a time. These raiders were the terror of the mountains, but Heracles fought them off. Not content with that, he spied out their hidden stronghold. It was a valley drained by just two narrow gorges cutting steeply to the sea. Heracles waited for a night of downpour and then blocked the gorges with great boulders, flooding his enemy out. The Minyan cavalry came after him over the narrow highland trails, only to be picked off, one at a time, by his poisoned arrows. This grim story has a happy ending, although long delayed. Archaeologists have identified the channels which the hero blocked, and engineers have cleared the boulders that dammed them up. So after its long punishment the Minyan land lies fair and open to the sunshine once again.

Crossing Arcadia, Heracles lost his way in a blizzard, and almost lost his life in the freeze that followed it. What saved him perhaps was the unprovoked attack of a wild boar. Red-eyed, bristling, the Erymanthian boar lies in wait for unwary travelers. He greets them with a rocketing rush from his den, slashing with the crescent knives of his snout. Squealing, he hooks for the groin. Thus he unmanned Adonis and many another hero, making their souls stream out in mingled gouts of blood and seed. But Heracles leapt to one side and ran lightly off, over the crusted snow, until the boar, intent upon pursuit, broke through the crust and wallowed helpless. Then Heracles whirled, leapt upon the floundering killer, and bound it fast. He was gasping and laughing both at once. The intense cold nipped his naked limbs less harshly now. In order to stay warm, he lifted the boar onto his back and staggered with it all the way into Erymanthos.

Later he came to the smiling plateau of Nemea. In its center is a double-mouthed cavern which the shepherds still avoid. A fearsome lion lived there in those days. The beast roamed as it pleased, feasting on flocks and men alike. Heracles now determined to destroy this bright lord of the dark. The difficulty was that no weapon made by man could pierce the monster. Heracles' poisoned arrows glanced harmlessly off its golden pelt. He used his club—and shattered it against those snarling jaws. Disdainfully, the lion turned away and paced back into its lair. So Heracles blocked up one entrance and went in himself at the other. He felt his way into the dripping heart of the mountain, down and down to the bloody chamber where his enemy lay growling like an earthquake. He saw the vertical green slits of the lion's eyes glowing in the dark. And now he knew what he must do. He flung himself straight forward, over the eyes, and clamped a stranglehold upon the lion from above. There followed an immense but brief explosion of fang and claw. Then the beast lay dead. Heracles dragged its carcass out to the light of day. He badly wanted the pelt, which no weapon of man could pierce, but how to cut it free? The lion's own claws, sharper than any steel, were his answer. He made it flay itself, in a sense. And for the rest of his life Heracles would wear the impervious lionskin as his own armor. He loosely knotted the forelegs across his chest and pulled the snarling muzzle up over his brow like a helmet.

Weapons of course are no use against dread. Moreover, dread inhabits a two-mouthed cave: the gut. It has to be met blind, deep inside oneself, and strangled there. Later it may be transformed into courage: the one armor that no weapon can pierce. So Heracles drew courage from the throat of dread. Just above his fierce blue eyes, the lion's eyes of inlaid jasper shone.

Some chroniclers, notably the poet Pindar, say that Heracles was physically smaller than average. That is most unlikely. However, an extremely well-knit man will always seem less than his actual size and weight because he is so concentrated, so "pulled together." According to the more common and reasonable accounts he was a big man, heavy-set but fast and hard. His feet were slender, quick and sure; he went barefoot the year round. His hands were finely formed, and yet the handshake of Heracles was something to avoid at all costs. This too involved a danger: if he thought himself snubbed, Heracles' jovial expression became rocklike, while his curly red beard seemed about to crackle into flame.

If Heracles' physical appearance was both admirable and frightening, so was his inner nature. He was passionately loyal, yet only a handful of heroes dared to call him friend. He was seldom chivalrous, yet women could never help falling for him. The general run of Heracles' contemporaries looked upon him with mingled fear, gratitude and awe. Their feeling is summed up in a line from Aristophanes: "Best not to rear a lion in the state, but, once he's reared, it's best to humor him." Just like a lion, Heracles moved often, slept in the open and feasted heavily. Men laughed at his gluttony (behind his back, of course) and yet strangely enough the only contest he ever lost was an ox-eating match at a country fair. Heracles laughed a lot himself, and cried too, as well and freely as a child. He boozed, bragged, bellowed and bawled. Meanwhile to cross him was to die, for mortal men.

Something had to be done about the stableyards of King Augeas. They had never once been cleaned, and their deep, steaming filth spread a pestilence throughout the countryside. So Heracles swore to get rid of it all. Here again, as in the Minyan fastness, he reconnoitered carefully before making his presence known. Then he went straight up to Augeas and announced that the morrow would be spring cleaning day. His proposition was to make the whole place spotless between sunrise and sunset. His price: one tenth of the king's cattle—or nothing if he failed. Better men than Augeas were to mistake Heracles' gusto for stupidity. Thinking to get a day's free labor from a muscular madman, the king sealed the bargain.

When Heracles promised a spring cleaning, he meant precisely that. Bright and early the next morning he dammed and diverted a mountain stream to make its white torrents tumble down through Augeas' property, sweeping everything loose out to sea. Clean-handed and unmussed, Heracles then broke his dam and returned the cataract to its proper plunging place. The noon sun dried and purified Augeas' grounds. What had been a brown miasmal purgatory was transformed into a setting of pastoral bliss. The birds sang; the cattle shone like new; men breathed again. Heracles, humming like a swarm of bees in his contentment, sauntered to the palace to collect. But Augeas himself was still dirty. He refused payment on the grounds that water, and not Heracles, had done the actual work. The hero, unpredictable as ever, let him off with that excuse.

Recent excavations in Israel throw a curious sidelight on this tale. It is now known that certain Old Testament communities were designed for just such cleaning methods as Heracles employed. Ingeniously devised aqueducts were built in to divert the neighboring streams right through each street and barn and even through some houses on the nights preceding holy days.

While he could never bear to bargain, or to press for the rewards his services merited, Heracles was not so averse to outright robbery. In this, as in many other virtues and vices, he remained a child of the age that bore him. Repenting of his softness to Augeas, he turned right around and resolved to revenge his honor in foreign parts, by rustling the red herd of Geryon, the King of the Golden West. This domain corresponded, apparently, to modern Portugal. Rumor insisted that Geryon ruled the kingdom in triplicate, as it were. He was endowed with three complete physiques, joined at the neck to a single regal countenance. This arrangement made Geryon a formidable fellow who feared no two-handed man, and he was certain to resist Heracles to the death. Geryon's very prowess and courage were to be his own doom, however, since they had served to attract Heracles' distant eye. Champions need outstanding opponents, and Geryon sounded worthy. Just to make the game more difficult, Heracles swore not only to defeat the king but furthermore to drive the red herd all the way back to Greece. These cattle, sleek and fleecy as a sunset cloud, were accounted the world's most desirable.

Heracles chose a surprisingly roundabout manner of getting his new adventure underway. He sailed first to Cyrene, on the green Libyan coast. From there he struck southward across a second, less hospitable sea: the Sahara Desert. He was making for what is now known as the Siwa Oasis: a lush little island of date palms, hard to find, no more than a single green dot amid the shifting and burning blankets of trackless sand. In those days it was called Ammon, a grove with an oracle sacred to Zeus. Ammon's beginnings had been lost in the mist of ages long before Heracles himself was born. The Oracle was felt to be the voice of Zeus himself. For these reasons, and despite the extreme difficulty of reaching it, the Oracle of Ammon ranked second only to Delphi's in the ancient world. There if anywhere, Heracles believed, he would learn at last the truth about his parentage. For he had heard that Zeus was his real father.

Even before Heracles arrived, he was granted a sign. Like

many another petitioner of Ammon, the athlete became hopelessly lost in the desert. He was dying of thirst when, furious at so meaningless a fate, he stamped his foot hard upon the ground. Where the sand lay dinted a cool spring instantly gushed forth. Refreshed by it, he found his way once more, and soon afterwards came stumbling into the presence of the god. To keep from blinding Heracles, radiant Zeus addressed him through a golden ram's-head mask. It is said that he acknowledged the hero as his natural son, fated to accomplish yet greater labors, to endure untold suffering and to become immortal.

Although this seems at first glance to be one of the least likely events in Heracles' career, it may well have happened almost precisely as told. Everyone knows the instinct of certain "diviners" for finding water in desert places. Heracles, whose life was so intimately bound up with water, may well have possessed that instinct. Moreover, in historic times Alexander the Great made a similar pilgrimage to Ammon which had a similar outcome. He too was lost and rescued on his way to the oasis by a "miracle" (this time attested by known witnesses) and it appears that the Oracle gave Alexander a similar reassurance of divine descent. Finally, the golden ram's-head mask through which the god addressed his son—or one just like it—has been found. It may be seen in the little museum at Aswan today. Of course, the Oracle was really devoted to the supreme Egyptian deity, the sun-god Ammon. The Greeks naturally equated Ammon with their own Zeus. And suppliants from other tribes used other names for him. None of that mattered to the keepers of the Oracle. They taught the supremacy of one god over all the earth; one god with many names. And they taught that all the best men on earth were sons of this one god—as Pharaoh was—destined for life eternal.

Following his dark encouragement by Zeus-Ammon, Heracles wandered back to the Mediterranean and took ship for Portugal. But at the Straits of Gibraltar, heavy seas and adverse winds combined to hold him back. This will come as no surprise to seafaring men; the Straits are still a dangerous bottleneck for running under sail. But Heracles was not one to acquiesce in idleness. As an aid to future navigation, and to while away the weeks he spent awaiting fair winds into the Atlantic, he built lofty towers for fire beacons on both the African and the European coasts. These "Pillars of Hercules" were to remain standing and in actual use well into Roman times.

While Heracles still labored at the Straits, news of his coming and his purpose were brought to King Geryon. The triple-giant could not but fume at such barefaced insolence, yet he found it amusing also. In his heart he too welcomed the struggle. Meanwhile it was for him to choose his weapons and the field, and furthermore, to arrange a suitably dramatic setting. He ordered first that the challenger's vessel be barred from the port, and Heracles alone brought off to shore, giddily spinning in a little gilded dinghy. The people were to welcome the hero in silence and mock mourning. A troop of weary old women, heavily veiled, were to escort him up the winding cliff road to the citadel and leave him alone at the last turning where the road ran straight on up to the iron gate. All that was done upon the fatal day. Heracles stood solitary in the middle of the sunny road, leaning on his club, before the gate. Silently it opened outwards.

King Geryon, armed cap-a-pie in his war chariot, came rattling out like a human threshing machine for threshing humans. Double-bladed battle-axes, each one sharp enough to draw blood from the wind, whined and flashed in all six of his hands. Not even Heracles could possibly stand up to such an onrush. So in the few seconds of grace that distance gave him, Heracles laid aside his club, strung an arrow, circled swiftly to one side, and shot: transfixing all three of Geryon's chests and hearts at once. The battle-axes shrapneled from the giant's hands, slashing up an acre of oak forest as he toppled and bumped, caught in the reins and dragged by his maddened horses on down the road to its first turning and straight on over the precipice into the gray

Atlantic Ocean far below. As down he sank, Geryon's writhing limbs seemed to take a new form; men say that he became a malevolent giant squid.

What followed may not be quite the longest cattle drive in history but it still stands among the most laborious. Heracles chose the coast of southern Europe for his route because however winding the way, it would be clear enough at all times: he had only to keep the sea on his right and stay with it, in order to reach home. At the Rhone Delta, hijackers attacked in force. He drove them off with a shower of stones, which supposedly accounts for the plain of fist-sized stones near the mouth of the Rhone today. During his needless detour of the entire Italian boot, Heracles built a mile-long causeway to get his cattle across a bay near Naples. Farther on he dug a lake to water them. Nearing home at last, he found his way barred by a river too deep and swift for the cattle to ford, so he dammed it up. He got his loot to Greece all right. Heracles may have been a little impulsive at times, but he was also indefatigable.

There are stories that prove him a towering toper besides, and no mean fornicator. He was natural man, spontaneous man, given mythic weight. Heracles forgot himself all the time; therefore his heart was pure. He stood empty of personal history, without the sense of sin, no guilt in him. Not because he had failed to do wrong—the truth is that Heracles did some abominable things —but because his path was no-path and his dread footstep light as air upon the wildflowers. No other hero ever accomplished half so much, nor planned so little. If he had any philosophy at all, it was antiphilosophical. Be yourself all the way, his actions say, and you may surprise yourself. You may become as strong as the storm wind, and as useful as the fructifying rain.

Until the fifth century before Christ, the Greeks revered him profoundly. But the full flowering of the classical culture was philosophical, political, esthetic, and brilliantly controlled at all points. The Greek playwrights saw Heracles afresh as violently comic or else tragic material. Sophocles—in *The Women of Trachis*—knocked him on the head. Euripides could be kinder— as in *Heracles Gone Mad*—but still very dark, troubled both for and about his hero. It seemed to such artists as these that Athens must be brought to a more balanced, just and reasonable view of the world than Heracles, as an ideal, could ever represent. Yet he remained the hidden spark, the bright spontaneous fire of romance, at the heart of Hellas.

Once and once only had Heracles sought to become wise. In Arcadia there lived a doe which had golden antlers like a stag. Antlers on a doe, like the horns of Moses and of Alexander the Great, signified something untoward, some secret power. What was it? Mighty sprouting horns stand for inspired thought? Then the mystery signified in all three cases was just wisdom. If I am right, then the doe's horns were the fairest twigs of the tree of knowledge, and the best prize that any huntsman could ever hope to take. The doe was a special pet of the goddess Artemis, virgin patroness of the chase, yet Heracles dared go after it. Week after week, month after month, he tracked his dappled prey. She was so shy, so swift. He trailed her all across Greece and up the steep Dalmatian coast. Finally at year's end he surprised her drinking from a stream near Venice. The moment had come, though he could not bear to injure her. Softly he drew an arrow from his quiver, aimed, and softly let fly. His arrow sped between the sinews of her forelegs, pinning them yet drawing no blood. Gleefully Heracles rose and ran up to the little thing. He laid hold of the antlers—when with the speed of thought Artemis swooped earthward to snatch away her pet.

Mere knowledge is obtainable treasure, but wisdom is a wild thing. One lays hold of wisdom for a moment, never longer. Instantly the Virgin Huntress swoops to reclaim her own. Then just as before the creature leaps and plays afar, a dappled doe racing the fragrant breezes at the world's edge. Sometimes, all unknowing, wisdom will slip away entirely, away past the wide gates of paradox. Yet her shadow has been seen there, waiting until wisdom turn, and return again. This very shadow offers much for hunters to imitate, if only we knew how to be so lowly, so playful and persistent in pursuit, so patient in separation. Holding her horned head high, one dainty hoof lifted from the turf, wisdom's sun-dappled shadow stands waiting at the gates. Meanwhile we course the valleys far below, now this way, now that way, on wisdom's fading, twining spoor, drawn on and on and on, dizzied with heart-hunger for her. Just this heart-hunger is the root source of the sense of search. Not only the quarry but the huntsmen too are creatures of the chase.

Returning empty-handed from his year-long hunt, Heracles heard of new adventure to the east. Troy was falling fast, attacked by a relentless water dragon. Immediately, Heracles marched to the rescue. No patriotic scruple barred the hero's way; the Trojan War was still to come. Arriving at the city after a series of forced marches, he held a hurried consultation with the trembling king and courtiers. Then he ordered the construction of a rampart to contain the monster, which was sleeping off a dinner of people. The next time it awakened and opened its great jaws, Heracles, who had been waiting sword in hand upon the parapet, leapt straight down the dragon's gullet, out of sight. Why the sword? That was never a part of Heracles' battle gear. As a public servant and champion of the oppressed he had always made a point of doing without aristocratic weaponry. He had found the plain club and bow, such as any peasant might carry in those days, quite sufficient for dealing with kings and monsters alike up to now. But this struggle would be different and it called for something new.

Even the tale of the Trojan Dragon seems to have had some basis in fact. The monster may well have represented a polluted well, the prime scourge of ancient cities in peacetime. Pollution brought plague, which could liquidate whole populations. That is why the ancients made a practice of abandoning polluted cities forever. Archaeologists have come across such sites, untouched by earthquake, fire, flood or war: cities that died intact and remained that way—with doors swinging open, fires laid, tables set and beds turned down with slippers under them—until old Earth accorded its own slow green burial to all. But rather than abandon their capital, the Trojans chose to trust in Heracles. Their city was destined for another sort of toppling, clangorous and bloody, brought by no dragon but a wooden horse, in days to come.

Heracles' first step, then, appears to have been the construction of a retaining wall around the entire neighborhood of the polluted well. Its purpose: to keep both animals and men clear of the infected area; also to minimize dangerous seepage of the poisoned waters into adjacent streets and cellars. This is still standard practice in such cases. The next step nowadays would be to dump truckloads of powerful dissolvents and disinfectants down the well itself, cleaning and sterilizing it by chemical means. Heracles lacked the necessary chemicals of course, and so he had to perform the crucial part of the work in person—scouring a live dragon's guts.

It must have shocked the Trojan gentry to see a shining weapon lowered to so menial a task, however dangerous. But a spade requires two hands, whereas Heracles had only one hand free. The sword served his purpose best. In his other hand he must have carried a torch, while a thick hawser, looped about his chest, became his life line to the world above. Occasionally he would call for fresh torches to be lowered on a second rope. Bread also came down when he called for it, along with some preventative medicine in the form of sour wine. Hour by hour he spiraled lower and lower down the sides of the black well, scouring with the sword as he descended to search out the dragon's black heart, the ultimate source of the plague. Not until he found it would Heracles emerge, for fear of polluting his fellows at the surface.

For the present he remained a pariah, exiled to the depths of earth. What with the ever-increasing darkness and the clamminess of the air as he descended, the work slowed more and more. Day passed into night and dawned again as he went down, shaving with his sword the bearded muck from every dribbling crevice. Sometimes, casting a torch end into the dark water below, he would catnap, swinging upright in his hawser, as a fresh torch swung down towards him like a slow-falling star. At last he reached the slimed surface and waded down through it, still scouring, as the water passed his ankles, his knees, his waist . . . Then suddenly his sword struck soft flesh. Sweating now, fearful for the first time in his life, he managed to impale the thing and raise it above water level to the light of his torch. It was a water-logged, green-rooted carcass, gleaming with phosphorescent growths.

Helpless in itself was this sodden and pustulent afterbirth of mortality, yet it sent hot and cold shudders through Heracles' hardy frame. He called for chains to be lowered. Scarcely daring to breathe, he got them wrapped around the thing and brought it safely up into the sunshine. The Trojans called it simply "the dragon's heart." Not one of them dared to go near enough to see precisely what it was, in fact, and Heracles himself never told. Perhaps it was only an infected calf or pig that had fallen into the well months previously, or it may have been the all-too-well-concealed corpse of a man murdered by poison, wreaking belated vengeance upon the entire city. Whatever it really was, Heracles bore his dripping burden to a hilltop far beyond the walls of Troy, and burned it to ashes on a blazing pyre. The next requirement was to purify himself. Heracles plunged deeper still into the woods, until he came upon a meadow divided by an icy stream. There he constructed a little hut of pine branches to serve as a sweat bath. He built a fire inside it, with flat rocks laid across the flames. As soon as the rocks began to glow, he poured cold water over them, steaming the dragon's breath from his limbs.

He had not come unscathed from the struggle. Tradition asserts that Heracles temporarily lost every hair of his head—pointing to a violent bout of fever which the sweat bath presumably cured. To complete the cure, he swam in the stream. Then, having rubbed himself down with olive oil and sand, he gave himself over to healing sleep at last.

At sunrise the next day he surprised a spotted deer drinking from the stream, shot it, and sacrificed it to Apollo, Averter of Plague. A grilled-venison breakfast completed his recovery, and Heracles retraced his steps towards Troy. It occurred to him to ask for some little reward as a token of his service and of the city's gratitude. The king's own chariot horses would do very nicely, he thought, being snowy white, splendid to see, and surpassingly swift to follow.

It so happened that the king of Troy thought much more of his chariot team than he did of Heracles. Secretly, sneeringly, he told his courtiers that the royal span was much too fine a gift to offer in return for what amounted to a sanitation job. On the other hand, Heracles did look as if he might be capable of violence when aroused. Troy's reputation for generosity had also to be considered. That reputation must be protected at all costs— short of the horses. After mulling this over, the king's ministers offered an alternative. Conceal the royal steeds; substitute a pair of ordinary white nags and present them as a most precious gift, accompanied by fanfare and fine oratory. The Trojans at court all assured each other and the king that Heracles would never know the difference.

The event proved them right, it seemed. Heracles sat through the speeches, graciously accepted the substitute horses' reins from the king's own hand, had the creatures hitched at once to his chariot, and drove slowly but grandly off into the sunset. He was actually cut to the quick, and therefore doubly careful to conceal the fact. As he rode away, the champion kept turning over in his mind a question which was to plague him all his life.

He was very far from being stupid or tasteless; his inmost principle, after all, was *noblesse oblige;* yet people constantly mistook him for a boor. Why? Heracles, like most misunderstood men, kept trying to find the answer in others, or in some general rule. Actually it lay very close to home. He was of the earth, earthy, with big appetites, blackened, broken fingernails, freckled shoulders and a gravelly voice. These things alone were quite sufficient to conceal his heroic nature, as in a cloud, from all snobs.

That same earthiness sets Heracles apart from other dragon-killers famed in song and story, such as Marduk, Indra, Perseus, Beowulf and Saint George. All these would seem to have personified forces of Light and Life in a single continuing struggle against Darkness and Death. In the abstract, Heracles also did that of course. But his earthiness and distinctness of personality, so typically Greek, have encouraged me to search for more concrete significance in each of his exploits. In the case of the Trojan Dragon, the shedding of Heracles' hair, as from a fever, offered one clue. His other struggles with water provided a strong context. And finally there was the fact that the classical world very often worshiped him as a god of health, hygiene and sanitation. For almost two thousand years the custom continued of carving a charm against disease over one's door, which ran: "Evil, keep your distance! Heracles is inside!" Doubtless my interpretation of the Trojan dragon story will strike some scholars as being "too ingenious." The same objection might be raised to my equally specific interpretations of certain other Heraclean exploits. To which I can only reply that when confronted with so individual, far-ranging and compelling a personage as Heracles it seems almost an act of piety to try to distinguish him from all the rest—and to rescue his deeds from the realm of generality.

The more he brooded on Trojan ingratitude, the more did Heracles feel inclined to punish it. So he pitched camp and slept on the problem. At dawn he awakened with blood still in his eye.

But gray-eyed Athena, daughter of the sky, seemed to be holding him back. As Heracles wrestled within himself, travelers from home appeared on the road ahead. They came urgently and then joyfully forward: here was just the man they sought. A menace even greater than the Trojan Dragon had all Greece in its grip, they reported. Flocks of cold misty creatures, ragged-winged, with icy, piercing talons, were rising from the marshlands round about Stymphalus to shadow the whole land with death. They flew forever beyond reach of Heracles' club; moreover they were far too many for his arrows to bring down. Yet Greece was praying that Heracles might somehow defeat the Stymphalian Birds.

What followed, hard upon the adventure of the Trojan Dragon, was almost equally gruesome and for much the same reasons. The pestilence he had to fight this time may actually have been carried by birds of the Stymphalian Marsh. Or perhaps mosquitoes, or the winds and clouds alone disseminated it from those cold and stinking waters, whose stream plunges deep underground and reappears at Miloi, ancient Lerna, by the sea. It is curious that Heracles was called upon to tame this hidden river twice over, first at Hydra, the murderously flooding outlet, and now again at Stymphalus, the stagnant source. This time his weapons were an ordinary spade, earplugs, and a pair of terribly loud brazen cymbals.

Savages in remote areas of the world still use shattering noise to drive away the "demons" of infection. Only Heracles, in his day, had the wit to take this ancient remedy out of the sickroom and carry it straight against the source of pestilence. Cymbals in hand, he circled the swamp, crashing out a skull-splitting din deliberately calculated to shatter the hearing organs of the birds. Terrified, they swarmed up from their nests, shrieking, and darkened the sun with their frenzied swoops and flutterings. Relentlessly Heracles kept on crashing, smashing and banging his brasses to create a steadily welling throb of sound. Thoroughly crazed at last, the birds dispersed to alien skies. Then Heracles cast aside his cymbals and took the plugs from his ears. As the last awesome thrumming died away, a skin-prickling silence descended, palpable as mist. Heracles shuddered, but he plunged into the marsh. Many hours of resolute floundering brought him to the weed-choked chasm that was its underground exit. Desperately hurrying to outpace the gathering darkness, he cut back the weeds and widened the chasm with his spade. Then he climbed a piece of high ground and built a bonfire to thaw out his ague-bitten body through the night. With thick sucking croaks and threatening lisps, the swamp retreated all night long around him, sweeping in upon itself and gradually drawing underground its miles-broad flotsam of birds' nests, water bugs, vipers and slime.

Most likely the Stymphalian Marsh was malarial. In any case, Heracles appears to have saved young Greece by draining it. Today the swamps are creeping back in around the lake, but not yet the birds of death.

There remains one story of Heracles' water-taming still to tell. This was a struggle for love's sake alone, and Heracles' opponent no mere slavering monster but instead an immortal god, Achelous by name, oldest of all rivers and yet ever-young; turbulent, silver-green, untamable. By preference Achelous usually inhabited a manlike form, though larger and more supple than a mortal's. From his man's brow sprouted two wide-curving horns. His beard streamed incessantly. His hands were like a concert pianist's: broad, long-fingered, clean, moist, restless, insatiable. His lean belly glistened with iridescent scales. Far beneath the river bearing his name Achelous' crystal palace gleamed, upholstered with soft mosses and ceilinged with mother-of-pearl. Carillons of troll-fashioned stream gold swung and sang in the foam about his belfries.

Invisible in a green dressing gown, Achelous reclined on his underwater terrace, idly combing the minnows from his shadowy hair as he watched the earth-maidens from what he called "the dry palace" innocently bathing and cavorting high above. The princess Deianeira was the loveliest of them all, when she dived like rosy quartz cleaving the green sky. Her chestnut hair licked and floated like a slick fiery cloak as lazily she arched away up again to sunlight, all unaware of his slow tossing horns.

She happened to be plagued with suitors, each one of whom considered himself the most eligible bachelor in Greece. Her light-footed tact did nothing to lessen their self-esteem, yet Deianeira cared not a whit for any of them. She loved her carefree maiden life: swimming, spinning, embroidering, hunting, daintily feasting, dancing and then swimming again the next day. Meanwhile, however, the suitors were eating her father out of palace and kingdom. Every man among them secretly believed that if only Deianeira were forced to pick a husband, the choice would fall upon himself. So they kept saying that she must. The poor king yielded finally, since there was nothing else for it. He sent heralds far and wide to announce that the princess would choose her own husband upon a certain morning not far off. In his heart the king was praying that yet one more suitor, somebody who really deserved his beautiful daughter, would appear on the appointed day.

It brought even greater suitors and more general excitement than the king had ever hoped to see. First Heracles appeared, hot from all-night marching, to claim the marriage prize. His fame was now immense, and the fear of him also. The more warmly he smiled the more his rivals' marrows froze with dread. One by one they deserted the contest, until he stood alone before Deianeira and the king. In a few minutes it would be noon, the marriage moment. Achelous meanwhile had risen to shore and dried himself as best he could. Now the god girded on his shimmering armor of pearls. Now he came sweeping grandly along past the palace and into the garden. He pushed into the silken pavilion where the princess and her father were entertaining Heracles. It astonished him to find only one other suitor, and that a burly, dust-streaked fellow in a lion's pelt. But what surprised him far more was that Heracles stood firm, a mere man against a god. In his thunderously gurgling voice, with mock courtesy, he inquired:

"Have I the honor of addressing glorious Heracles?"

"At your service, O divine Achelous."

"You are dull, Heracles, yet surely not quite so presumptuous as to set your strength against my immortal waters! Leave us; learn to play by yourself! Go bathe, at least!"

"Better for you, Achelous, dripping one—bull-headed, weed-haired, sneeze-torn, mud-foot garbage collector that you are at best—to treat more humbly with a son of Zeus! My club is quick!"

"And my fish are fresh, fellow! You call yourself a son of Zeus, yet your mother was a mortal, married to Amphytrion of Thebes. So you're either a liar or—"

Grinning, but with gritted teeth, Heracles shrugged out of his lion's pelt and lightly cast his club aside. It seemed for just a moment that Achelous hesitated; some streams have second sight. But then he slipped off his pearly raiment and stood naked also: huge, silent, threatening, with lowered horns.

Deianeira crouched close against her father's knee. Her tearful blue gaze flickered, now soft, now filled with fear, between the two towering contestants.

Suddenly Heracles dashed to crash his boulder-like shoulders hard against the iridescent belly of the god and bring him down doubled over gasping like a cataract. They rolled locked together in choking dust. The whole bright garden shook its colors loose. Wide horns were rising, and Deianeira screamed. But Heracles rose also, fast-grappled still to the god; swaying as if in time to slow music, a dance of death, he lifted Achelous clear of the ground, squeezing until blood burst from the god's broad nostrils to stain their mingled beards. In a wink Achelous narrowed all over to cable slimness, turned slick and slipped hissing from Heracles' grip. A quicksilver serpent he slithered, looped, contracted to a glittering coil, slit-eyed, fork-tongued, spitting threat of instant death. As the creature reared to strike, Heracles sprang and caught it tight about the gullet, crushing its metallic scales and moist cold flesh together in his eager fingers as he cried out gleefully, shaking his enemy:

"I knew snakes in my cradle, Achelous! At Lerna I cut down a whole tree of serpents! You don't frighten me!"

But the god swelled and lurched loose from Heracles' stranglehold, snorting: a huge black bull now, foam-flanked, daintyhoofed, his round eyes alight with more than animal malice as he charged. Barely slipping that first murderous rush, Heracles closed with the bull as it swung about. He reached under the neck to seize the far horn in both hands, then desperately but still deliberately twisted it back, minute by minute, his knuckles white on the white horn while the beast bellowed in agony. Gradually he wrenched its head back chin-to-sky. At the moment of utmost strain he silently invoked his heavenly father and then flung his full weight furiously down upon the down-pointed horn, driving it deep into the ground and snapping it clean off. The bellowing of Achelous abruptly changed to human groans and bitterly repentant words. Resuming the shape of a horned man—but with only one horn now—he acknowledged defeat.

Achelous proved a gallant loser, and Heracles accordingly honored him as best man at the wedding. The river-god brought along a present which seemed a small thing at first sight, a thoughtful souvenir and nothing more: the horn broken off by Heracles. But no sooner had Deianeira accepted the gift and warmed it for a moment between her two hands than it started overflowing with flowers and the sweet fruits of spring. This was to be the legendary Cornucopia, inexhaustible.

Men have naturally gone on dreaming of the Cornucopia. It was no dream, however, but a promise—a promise of the plenty that tamed rivers can and will provide. The most lastingly momentous labor that Heracles ever undertook was to seize this horn for the uses of mankind. There can be no abiding mystery about the Cornucopia, once it is considered in the context of Heracles' other water-taming exploits. It stands for irrigation; it represents the channel broken off from the mainstream of a river to insure rich harvests even in dry summer weather. Drought and famine fall before this fabulous horn, the wedding gift of lovelorn, thrice-defeated Achelous, and Heracles' noblest trophy.

One yet greater offering did Heracles bring to all the ages and all the world, an idea that has worked and will work a transformation of humanity itself. This really won immortality for Heracles: the determination to be heroically of use. He thirsted for renown through service. And the name of Heracles lives because he lived up to it.

Towards the end of his life Heracles plunged from Cape Malea deep into the sea. He groped his way down to a green doorway in the sea floor. This he entered, quickly closing the door behind him against the water's weight. Far below spiraled a stairwell of obsidian, lit by diamond outcroppings. He followed this down to a second door, a trap door in the rigid sky of Hades. So he dropped through into that shadowy realm. The king there—he of the many guests—greeted Heracles hospitably enough. "I know your mission," the king said. "It is to borrow Cerberus, my watchdog. You'll recognize him by his three heads." Heracles, naked and alone, went searching through the high halls. At last he came to the Throne of Death, and saw the gaping jaws in the shadow beneath it. Reaching in, he seized forth Cerberus. He collared him. He dragged the frenzied monster all the way home to the light of day. Then at a sunny crossroads he let Cerberus go. At once a chasm opened to receive the creature. Cerberus, yelping with relief, plunged out of sight. The past, the present and the future were contained in those three heads of Cerberus.

By dragging the dog to daylight, Heracles had stopped time itself —for an hour.

The cosmos is a paradoxical tapestry, woven on a beating loom. The very beating of the loom obscures it. By his last labor Heracles held back the beating of the loom, the beat of blood in his own temples, and the beating of the waves against Cape Malea. What saw he then?

Deep earth had blessed his beginnings with beneficent serpents. A dark sky blessed his end. Enveloped in the fires of a poisoned cloak which he could not tear off, knowing that he must die, Heracles heaped up his own funeral pyre at the top of Mount Ossa. He built the pyre in agony, yet once it was lit he lay serene within the jovial blaze. And when his hard, laborious flesh had been consumed altogether away, Father Zeus sent a thunderbolt to burn up the very bones as well. Instantly the soul of Heracles leapt along the lightning bolt's obedient return, home to his father's throne. Thereafter he would tread the Milky Way; he would wrestle with streams of stars, and harry the frost-bristled beasts from distant galaxies. He would warm his hands at fires beyond our sun.

Heracles had never claimed to be a god on earth. He was passionately human, serviceable, direct. But Earth became his steppingstone to godhood. Heracles showed what one man can do. He earned divinity.

ONE GLASS OF RAKI

COME AND JOIN ME at the Piyer Loti Café for half an hour. It is almost dusk. We are at the moment when the day goes into reverse; gold cools to silver and the silver swiftly tarnishes to darkness. Our drink will be the many-named potion of the Mediterranean shores: pernod, pastisse, anis, ouzo—raki, they call it here. Add a little water to what seemed water in your glass, and milky clouds obscure it. Drink but two or three of these dusk distillations and a slender silver hammer strikes once at the base of the brain.

Waters, moving waters, are the hair, beard, mantle, eyes and crown of all this place. Cool sweet springs surround it. Flowing fountains abound inside it. A salt stream pours past it. A silver sea spreads before it. A deep harbor divides it. The waters are shimmering with delicious fish, laden with the slow dance of great ships and small.

Inland cities make one think of landlocked ships, or riverboats too swollen to pass downstream. They too experience the tides of trade and they too are temporary havens for the wandering man. But where water thrusts deepest in a city, she will be most loved. Water makes Manhattan Island sparkle like a diamond under the tap. It laps the French lace and cocoa of Port-au-Prince. It puts quicksilver in the dark folk of Rio. It waits chimney-high by Rotterdam. It giggles in the bosom of Marseilles. It softly washes liquid fossil Venice. And it glitters far below us now.

We sit amid the privacy of death. The Piyer Loti is a three-table cafe at the top of a hill heavy with tilted and turban-carved headstones. The cemetery slopes straight down from our knees to the Golden Horn. There fleets of galleons used to valley safe. But now the Horn is sheathed with stinking docks, slums and industrial muck. The sheath festers, although the blade be God-renewed forever. Our glance sweeps the Horn's five miles of narrow water to the Bosphorus, and the far-gleaming Sea of Marmara. By them rises the ancient town, mother-of-pearl at this distance, dreamlike. But the metropolis has proved intensely solid, gleaming with heavenly and also hellish lights for more than three thousand years. She destroyed the pagan world. Also, she brought the Christian world into being. Half our history begins at the Horn.

The city was first Lydian, then Greek, then Roman-ruled. Her great millennium began when the Emperor Constantine made her the Rome of the East. In the year 330 he walked around the town, dragging the point of his spear. He was tracing out new fortifications for the capital that would bear his name. His gen-

erals trailed after him, anxiously taking notes. His building plan
seemed much too ambitious. At last an aide found courage to ask
the emperor where he meant to halt. Constantine replied, as if in
rapture: "When He who leads me tarries." That set the tone
for a thousand years. In each succeeding emperor's council chamber was an empty throne, ostensibly intended for Christ the Lord.
Idealism and cynicism waged constant battle for that seat. A
New Testament lay before it, open always, as a sort of Constitution. Since the Book of Revelations describes a New Jerusalem
built all of purest gold, Constantinople pressed towards that bi-
zarre condition too. At the height of its power the Byzantine
capital had five hundred churches, each one with a golden dome.
The coinage also was of gold. It showed the reigning emperor's
visage on one side, and Christ on the other. Church and State
stood back to back by the Horn. Together they proved unshak-
able, for century after century. Meanwhile a drink more powerful than raki maintained the city's youth and loveliness intact.
The ingredients of this magic brew were human blood, gold dust
and salt water.

On Coronation Day each emperor accepted a sack of human
ashes from the bishop. To pay for it he strewed gold coins upon
the altar. Thereafter he occupied a gold-filled world. Even his
choice of a bride was solemnized with gold. The most desirable
maidens of Byzantium used to line up for inspection in the emperor's palace. And he would pass among them, blushing, peering, clutching a golden apple in his hand. At one such bride show
the Emperor Theophilus halted before a radiant young creature
named Cassia, who was admired as a budding poet. Dubiously,
and rather rudely, he recited in Greek: "A woman brought mankind to sin." Cassia, smiling, at once completed the couplet with
a line of her own: "And woman brought salvation in." She meant
that if Eve was female so was the Virgin Mary. Theophilus
quickly moved on. He gave the golden apple to a simple-seeming,
pious and delicious little wench named Theodora. Tambourines

and cymbals sounded at their wedding feast, while choirs of eunuchs chanted:

> *"I have taken the flowers of the field*
> *and laid them with fervor in the nuptial chamber.*
> *I have seen the new-wed couple,*
> *sunlike, on a couch of precious gold.*
> *Roses for those who are lovely as the rose!*
> *Joy to the golden pair!"*

The throne room also was a golden sanctuary, designed to over-awe. It was octagonal, with deep shadowy niches in each side and a vast dome above. Its incense clouds were illuminated by hundreds of candle flames reflected in crystal chandeliers. The floor, of many-colored marbles and mosaics, was guarded by mechanical creatures of gold. As the foreign ambassador or suppliant entered, fierce golden griphons lifted their crimson-inlaid beaks at his throat, shrieking and whistling. When he reached the inner circle, golden lions rose up to roar at him. Then utter silence fell, more terrible still, and loneliness. Slowly, the incense cleared. Like sunshine, a liquid singing sifted from above. It was a little jeweled bird, perched high among the branches of a golden plane tree growing from the floor. And close beneath the bird, gently swinging in state upon a golden, mid-air throne, sat the emperor. He had manifested himself; he might even deign to blink; but not a single word was said.

William Butler Yeats expressed a yearning to be like the Byzantine emperor's mechanical songbird, taking

> *. . . such a form as Grecian goldsmiths make*
> *Of hammered gold and gold enameling*
> *To keep a drowsy Emperor awake;*
> *Or set upon a golden bough to sing*
> *To lords and ladies of Byzantium*
> *Of what is past, or passing, or to come.*

Naturally, that half-miraculous songbird has long since flown. Gold, although it is untarnishable, keeps getting melted down and being given new forms. Much of the faceless bullion in state treasuries was once crowns, coins, sculptures, necklaces, sceptres, crucifixes and princes' toys. Lasting art is apt to be of humbler materials. Among the ancient sculptures far more bronze than gold survives, more stone than metal, and more clay than stone.

The pagan world produced enormous quantities of art; Byzantine policy destroyed most of it. The Emperor Theodosius was one who gave orders that the great pagan temples be pushed over, and their images melted down. What remained was quarried for Byzantine building purposes. The Emperor Justinian ransacked Europe, Asia and Africa for columns, capitals, pavements and panelings of rare marble, porphyry, basalt and onyx. He stripped enemy palaces of gold and silver, exotic woods, crystal, silk and precious stones. All these were to adorn the noblest basilica ever seen. To begin at the bottom, its basement was a pillared cistern the size of a small lake. Water pumped up into the church flowed steadily over egg-shaped marble fonts. The interior construction called for archway piled upon archway, glimmering with reflected lights and colored shadows, rising, rising to a vast and cloudy dome. It was like a transparent parasol lifted against downpouring jewels. Something of the cosmos seemed to rest within it, as the human skull may enclose an infinity of thought. They named the church Aghia Sophia, "Holy Wisdom." The Parthenon, its loveliest elder sister, had also been dedicated to Wisdom. And these two temples proved to be mother vines for the marbled arbors of mankind. Most of our great buildings hark back to either one or the other. Architecture at its height has their living emptiness, mental masonry, music of the mind which brick and stone obey.

Justinian dedicated Aghia Sophia with a brag: "Glory be to God who has thought me worthy . . . I have vanquished thee, O Solomon!" Pious legend holds that the emperor sprang to heaven on the strength of this accomplishment alone. Things in the nearby Hippodrome were less than heavenly. In fact all the enormities which had made the Roman Colosseum infamous were being repeated there. Now the torturing and burning of so-called heretics was carried on by Christians themselves. The greatest evils are done in the name of the greatest good. Constantinople alternately mothered and smothered a multitude of Christian sects. The dread of her "Satanodrome" drove hundreds of thousands of unorthodox citizens into voluntary exile. And so the paradoxical fabric of Christianity spread across Europe.

As the centuries went by, Constantinople's own territories shrank and shrank, almost to the circuit of her walls. Yet she still held her empire economically. The world had never known such mercantile magnificence as hers. Chian wine, Egyptian grain, Armenian caviar, Thracian cattle, Russian furs and dried fish of the Bosphorus were traded along the Horn. But gold, silver, silk and precious stones became the city's primary concern. Raw treasure was unloaded every day onto her docks, and luxury objects departed. Constantinople was a paradise of artisans, a golden honeycomb beside the salt sea road. It is said that a third of the world's transportable wealth stood within her walls at one time.

Her defenses included a "Barbarian Office" which recruited and deployed undercover agents throughout the known world. Their main function was to stir up trouble between Byzantium's rivals. Their methods included slander, assassination and lavish expense-account giving. Consider this typical bribe to a certain minor sultan. Twice each day for eighty days they sent him a banquet. Each time the gold and silver tableware remained in his possession. Had he dared return his dirty dishes, poison would have been employed instead.

The city's immediate safety rested in the mailed fists of its mercenaries. They came from far corners of the Earth to serve the Prince of Peace, bringing their own heathen idols, priests, interpreters and chefs in train. One thing that drew them to

Byzantium was the gay life on the world's most cosmopolitan waterfront. Another was the offer of privileged, tax-free status. But the great magnet of course was the enormous pay in gold. The emperor's officers got up to forty pounds of the stuff annually, and booty too. His personal bodyguard consisted, by the way, of Bedouins, Scythians, Iberian slingers, yellow-bearded Britons, axe-hurling Celts, Russians "as tall as palm trees," slant-eyed Slavs, and finally the fur-clad, horn-helmeted Vikings, who were dreaded everywhere. These last were living heroes of Norse sagas in the making. They smelled of fish and balsam, and swore by thunderous Thor. Constantinople was to show up often in the sagas as Milkegarde—"White Bastions"—a distant land of sunshine, opportunity and freedom from care.

Byzantium's good times ended when it tried to play host to the Fourth Crusade. This was a mighty expedition of Frankish knights, commanded by the Counts Katznellenbogen, Blois, Flanders and Montfort. Venice financed it, and transported it by water as far as the Bosphorus. The great land assault southward against the Saracen was supposed to start from there. But the Venetians had an altogether different end in view. They wanted Constantinople's trade empire for themselves, and the Venetian merchants had long since learned the Byzantine art of double-dealing for state purposes. Now they deliberately picked a quarrel with Constantinople, and bribed the chief crusaders to back their cause. Negotiations were begun and sabotaged by Venetian guile. Like some fabulous blind water dragon on a golden halter, the expedition encircled the city walls. Closer coiled the dragon. It reared up, clawing, and the white bastion broke. This was Christendom's most suicidal moment. Constantinople was laid open for three full days and nights of wild pillage. Her people were decimated, and the heaped-up treasure of a thousand years was clawed to shreds. Not since the world began, wrote the noble Geoffrey de Villehardouin, had there been so rich a haul. He was right.

Soldiers piled their pack animals with silk, ermine and silver fox, services of silver and gold, and sacks of precious stones. Chalices, altar cloths and vestments heavy with gold were swept from all five hundred churches. The more pious plunderers confined themselves to holy relics, encased of course in jeweled reliquaries. A large part of this loot remains today in European churches. Halberstadt fell heir to the Head of Saint James, Amalfi drew the Body of Saint Andrew, and Pisa the Head of Saint John Chrysostom. Bromholm in England obtained a sizable splinter of the True Cross, and Sens in France collected the Crown of Thorns. Soissons struck it rich with the Forefinger of Doubting Thomas, the Head of Saint Stephen Protomartyr and the Head of Saint John the Baptist. Amiens had to make do with a second Head of John the Baptist. While these curiosities survived, innumerable masterpieces of art were destroyed. Only the sly Venetians looted with taste. Home to their own water-city went shiploads of lovely things, including the gilded bronze horses that adorn St. Mark's Cathedral still. The best minds and hands of Byzantium also went west in the service of their conquerors. These displaced persons were to set the stage for brutal Europe's coming Renaissance. Meanwhile Constantinople, bled white, would stumble on alone against the rising Moslem tide.

When Ottoman Turks overwhelmed her in 1453, the city was locally renamed Islam-Bol, for "Many Moslems." Within a century she ruled a great empire, extending from the walls of Vienna to the passes of Afghanistan. Suleyman the Magnificent, and his Admiral Barbarossa, practically controlled the Mediterranean. Europe feared and courted the sultans. Good Queen Bess sent one of them a present: a pipe organ equipped with mechanical singing blackbirds.

Istanbul, as the Ottomans called it, kept up its own extravagant traditions. But with Oriental touches added. When Prince Mehmet the Third was introduced to his people at the Hippodrome, he wore knee breeches of gold-embroidered satin—and also a single enormous emerald earring. Black heron feathers nodded in his turban. He carried a rock-crystal mace. Among his showier presents were four giraffes, nine elephants, eleven storks, seventeen lions, nineteen leopards, twenty-one camels, twenty-two horses, twenty-five falcons and, to top the bill, nine sirens. But this whole life-size menagerie was made of sugar candy. Such festivities occasioned grand parades as well, in which every professional guild took part: arrow-makers, nightingale-dealers, tumblers, bear-trainers with their shuffling charges, stark-naked pearl-divers, tripe-cooks, asylum-keepers leading long files of lunatics in chains, the eighty licensed and litter-borne coffeehouse bards, night watchmen with torches, shouting "Stop Thief!" and, last but not least, the Lord High Executioner with his train, carrying seventy-seven separate instruments of persuasion, chastisement and death.

The Seraglio, the old Sultan's Palace, was built near the Hippodrome, on a high point of land overlooking the Sea of Marmara. Four or five thousand subjects lived at the palace. Luckiest among them were the pageboys, kidnapped from Europe. These got a fourteen-year education of the utmost quality and rigor, based on Plato's *Republic*. They grew up to be Janizaries, philosophic warriors who ran the empire in the sultan's name. His harem was less fortunate: a thousand or more tender prisoners kept and fattened for his possible, and sole, enjoyment. The white-skinned keepers of these "fresh flowers" were partially castrated, and their black guards wholly so. Boredom ruled the harem more than any man could have done. Indiscretions naturally followed. But all captured lovers were sewn into sacks and heaved headlong from the battlements, into the shuddering sea.

In the nineteenth century the court passed from its medieval palace to a plush and crystal confection on the waterfront. Istanbul was holding back from the modern world, and slowly losing everything except romance. Bismarck sent a jeweled beer stein to the sultan, but he never bothered to open mail from Istanbul.

With the First World War the old regime expired. Then Mustafa Kemâl and his "Young Turks" took over. They bibulously battered into shape a European-style nation on the Bosphorus. Now the city turns "modern." The camel is fled from her streets, although not yet the dolphin from her waters. Smart clean cats and dirty pigeons patrol the cobblestones. Children sail toy boats in the fountains and play hopscotch amid the fallen leaves. They have a touching seriousness, as of children in books. Or as if each boy and girl were hoping to find a treasure beyond price, hidden somewhere nearby. The Great Roc's diamond egg, perhaps, or the stone than can turn anything to gold, or even Aladdin's wonderful lamp. Not having seen such things on television, they still believe in them. At the same time, since they live mostly on the streets, the kids know pretty well how the world goes. They frown slowly, as if remembering. And smile swiftly, forgetting again. Their city contains much to remember, along with some things that might better be forgotten.

In mid-April the storks come winging in from Africa. They circle and salute the metropolis before dispersing, each to his own summer tree or chimney. In October they depart with equal ceremony. Nature, like the storks, seems reluctant to desert so pearly a pasture. The Earth here is no dank backyard sprite but a great Mother which the city necklaces. The ancient fortifications are green-plumed, "branchy between towers." Forests murmur almost at the gates. The air is of a wet silver sheen. Songbirds still outchoir the *müezzins* in their minarets and the cocks too are clocks. The sun is amber, as often as not, gleaming through rain clouds of smoky quartz. "Nature and the mosques," as the citizens say, are Istanbul's delights.

The mosques can be as intimate as tents, or as expansive as a sky hung out to dry. Like an early-morning homecomer one tiptoes, shoes in hand, across a threshold onto warm-colored carpets and into a kaleidoscope. Then slowly the carpets, columns, tiling and inevitable dome combine to create a world poised between nature and art: a geometrical garden grove. Instead of an altar, there is an inlaid prayer niche, lit by a starry lamp. For Moslems this becomes a narrow opening on seas of stars.

Christian tradition tells of a juggler who, thinking himself clumsy at prayer, amused the Virgin Mary with his tricks instead, performing alone at night before her altar. She was pleased. Moslems pray with the body also; they perform what amounts to a still-centered dance of worship, with many, many prostrations and with lovely quiet gestures of the hands and head. Besides being a beautiful discipline this is rather a formidable one, which must in itself go far to make the body a firm vessel for the soul. The brooding stranger who watches motionless from his flying carpet, so to speak—in but not of this worship—may yet be moved by it. Finally the actual service begins, with cage-shattering chants of exaltation: unutterably splendid and strange.

Strolling at random after the service, one threads the Street of Typists: silent men with portables set on upended soapboxes under the trees, ready to put a lease, a longing or a curse on paper. Clients perch sideways to the typists, on camp chairs, bending to murmur as if in the ears of priests. One comes to the Spice Market: drab booths of bureaus, the bureau drawers stuffed with the kitchen treasures of the Orient—*Yenibahar, Biber, Somak, Kimyon.* Over by the Galata Bridge, Toonerville trolleys, sultan-red in the sunlight, spill tea-colored Turks hurrying in all directions. In five minutes the ferry leaves for Asia. It is tempting to go out upon the water, and with luck one may find a magician aboard. He seemed a hulking old stevedore until—*abracadabra!*—there went your watch. He swallowed it; he digs it out again through a hole in his shirt. Now, giving and receiving, he draws two lumps of sugar from a schoolgirl's nose. She grins wide as a pie while the conjurer passes casually on. He goes fluttering and tromping like some elephantine butterfly, weaving tiny mysteries between the continents.

The patron saint of Istanbul is Sherif Eyüp, boon companion

to the Prophet. In the course of an early and ill-fated seige he was killed outside the city walls. His tomb stands where he dropped. Turks call it the most sacred spot on earth after Mecca. Here cocks and lambs are sacrificed, and seemingly miraculous cures occur all the time. Just outside the green doors of Eyüp's mausoleum there stands a hollow tree, centuries old, reserved for disabled storks. An alley starts nearby, dips and begins climbing. It turns into stairs, mounting between the walls and then the roofs of houses. It passes higher, along a green hillside crenelated with headstones, and comes at last to the Piyer Loti Café.

Here we sit talking, finishing our raki, while Istanbul darkens at our feet: water, iron, mother-of-pearl, minarets, fish, flowers and fair glances and water, always water, all folding together now into night.

THE ASTONISHING SCALLOP

SOME TRAVELERS greet even the dawn with indifference—as if returning a blank stare. While granting that "natural" men may welcome you, nature herself (they say) does not. Remember the howler monkeys. And while closing your ears against them, try not to step on a fer-de-lance! Nature does seem jagged and torn, so often. Yet she does work together as one thing, of course. Like the legendary pelican which tore open its own breast to feed its young. Nature works to welcome life, one's own included. And life also is a journey. This point was underlined for me not long ago in conversation with a game warden from

Uganda. I asked him what his main job was, and he replied: "Preserving the natural balance; doing nothing! Every wild thing, without exception, lives to benefit all the rest. Not even a mosquito should be disturbed by us. My problems are not rogue elephants and all that so much as sentimental riflemen and nice old chemists!"

Casting about for a more natural villain I mentioned crocodiles. "Delighted," he cried. "Delighted you brought them up! Crocs will grab off a bather or a fisherman now and then. Used to happen quite frequently in one of the Nile lakes. So they shot out all the crocs along there. As a result, the pikes which had been the crocs' chief nourishment went and multiplied like mad. The pikes ate all the plump little perch in the process. This perch was the villagers' staple diet. They're starving now. . . . And so it goes. There are more villainous-seeming things than crocs, anyhow. Take wild dogs. They move in voracious packs, striking terror wherever they appear, causing a continual stampede. At leisure they'll pick off some panting great bull, the head of the herd. Hard on him, very. But meanwhile the entire animal life in his district has been revitalized. The stampede brings new pastures, new partners and new leaders to light."

Nature is sometimes terrifying, but never vicious. That was his conclusion. Practically everyone who lives close to nature says the same. Obviously nature cannot welcome all things at once. Each individual must take its turn with her, its own time of life. This gives death a great deal to do. Death is the frantic stage manager, that's all. Still . . . death comes hard as a rule. The mere idea of death can be profoundly troubling. Is that why we keep on thinking about it?

The elephant faces death alone, with dignity and apparent equanimity. He lies down in a shady place where other elephants before him have been wont to die. He says goodbye to his friends. Regretfully they leave him living there alone. His last few days are solitary, practically motionless, brooding alone, like some gray knoll of mist fading motionless away into the morning air.

The beasts have taught men virtue. The human tribes of earth do very often practice the lion's fearlessness, the eagle's aspiration, the bull's directness, the dog's loyalty, the lark's lightheartedness, the elephant's patience. Beyond their particular qualities the animals all live and die with a certain inherent grace. This too we try, despairingly sometimes, to emulate. But is there any animal at all who teaches hope? It would help, for many and many a one of us lacks this.

Consider the lowly scallop. He is small and weak and seldom seen except at table. People know him for a tasty shellfish. They vaguely guess that he cavorts in billions below the surface of the ocean, and that is all. Yet the scallop used to be reckoned among the most mysterious and grand of all created things. Moreover, from the Stone Age until just the other day he exercised a profound and pervasive influence upon mankind. In his small, peaceful, silent and subaqueous way the scallop swam deep into human consciousness and established a second home there. Remember "The Birth of Venus"? Botticelli's masterpiece in the Ufizzi Gallery in Florence is a glory to see, still dewy-fresh as when it was put to dry five centuries ago. Venus stands nude, at ease and gently smiling, and her red-gold hair streams out upon the April breezes that are hastening the goddess shoreward over the bluegreen sparkling bay. Her boat is a scallop shell, as it happens, and this seemingly insignificant fact points to just one of many climactic events in the scallop's amorous and mystical career.

A hundred and fifty million years ago, when the Sierra Nevadas first boiled up out of the ground, and the Pacific Ocean rolled over Washington and Oregon, then the scallop was young. Dinosaurs wallowed screaming in the rivers. The first bird spread its wings, fell and survived. There were a few tiny mammals also. Trumpetings as faint as elfin horns might have led one to the romping ground of elephants no larger than mice. But man himself would have to wait another hundred and forty-nine million years or so to be born. By then the scallop already commanded an immeasurable kingdom. Chemistry gives a startling clue to the extent of the shellfish world: while rivers are very rich in calcium, the ocean itself yields hardly a trace of it. The reason being that shellfish appropriate practically all the calcium in the sea to fashion their own armor. The powdered remains of their shells cover the bottom of the ocean in layers up to two miles thick. Shellfish built the white cliffs of Dover. The Temple of Zeus at Olympia was constructed of great blocks of petrified shellfish, especially the scallop.

Children at the beach can often see the small fry of the scallop skipping about in tidal pools. Tiny creatures with frail, transparent shells, they busily do somersaults, barrel-rolls, spins, loop-the-loops, power take-offs, glides, dives and yard-long zigzags through the still water. Far out of sight in the depths, hand-size parent scallops are practicing similar feats, and making long migrations besides. Here is the scallop's first mystery. How can he, with neither fins nor tail, and without so much as stirring from his shell, swim so nimbly? Jet propulsion is his secret. First he sucks in all the water he can hold, then he claps his shell shut, tightly compressing the muscles along its inside edges and jetting water in any direction or combination of directions he desires. Repeating the maneuver in staccato rhythm, he moves forward, back, up, down or sidewise with all the agility of a flying saucer.

There are well over a hundred and fifty species of this animal. He swarms along the coasts of every continent except Antarctica, and his multitudes are incalculable. Yet it takes some diving to surprise a real live grown-up scallop at home. Frighten him and he will jet away. But if one approaches very gently he will just close down his shell to a thin slit and lie there peering. His eyes—up to a hundred of them—twinkle through the deep like a bracelet of tiny blue diamonds set in black. They are the living scallop's most unforgettable feature.

Otherwise he looks more neat than spectacular: like a corrugated castanet. The corrugations, raying out from the hinge at the back, lend strength to a shell built for lightness. Crossing them are concentric rings which show his age, like the rings of a tree. When he has grown accustomed to your presence, the shell opens somewhat and thousands of miniature tentacles emerge to form a wavering crown about an inch high. With this crown he smells, touches, tastes and feeds, tonguing in microscopic bits of life.

Firmly self-imprisoned, having just his retractable crown of tentacles for contact with the outside world, how can the scallop possibly reproduce his own kind? Like so many of nature's best-kept secrets, the answer is really very simple. Each individual scallop is hermaphroditic, blessed with both male and female reproductive glands. At the time of the full moon the glands co-operate to produce semi-transparent eggs the size of dewdrops. Released into the encircling sea, these almost invisible galleons of the race soon rise to the surface and vanish like bubbles, releasing in their turn a new generation of scallop: glassy, miniscule and spry.

Our ancestors had no way of deciphering this. When men of old watched the new scallop appear on full-moon nights, he seemed to be arising straight from the luminous foam. As late as the sixteenth century they still described him as "a shelfishe engendered of the Ayre and dew." No wonder he was reverenced! A creature who swims without visible means, has a hundred shining eyes, and comes into existence spontaneously through the action of wind, waves and moonlight alone—what could be more mysterious?

In the days when the first human beings clung shivering to the marshy shore, the scallop began to exert his legendary pull upon human thought. The people of that time were not hunters but hunted, penned between the devil and the deep blue sea. They hid out along the edges of the salt flats, where heavier carnivores could neither smell nor follow them. Their own diet consisted of shellfish, including the scallop, almost entirely. Generation after generation, while man was screwing up his courage to move in-land, the unceasing tides continued to lay this monotonous banquet gently at his feet. He owed his life to the sea, the shellfish, and their scallop king. Archaeologists have deduced these facts about mankind's modest start in life from the so-called "kitchen middens" of northern Europe. Ancient headlands of shells salted through with flint knives and other human relics, these middens are all that remain of innumerable beach picnics, rich in scallop. They contain no direct evidence of actual scallop-worship. But there is abundant evidence of such worship in a later stone age, miraculously preserved on our own shores.

When Columbus discovered America, he opened up a civilization that was intensely religious but still ignorant of the wheel and of all metals except silver and gold. The highly cultivated Indians of Central America used swords and fish hooks of obsidian. Among their chief divinities was Chalchiuhtlicue, "She of the Jade Skirt." Her domain was the jade-green sea, from which she sometimes rose waist-high. Her husband was the rain-god Tlaloc. It happens that the priests of her cult set scallop shells at their shoulders and over their hearts. Moreover, Indian maidens were wont to wear a single scallop shell suspended at the hips. Why scallop shells and not some other kind? A certain clay vessel from ancient Peru gives the key to this enigma. Its body is a scallop and its spout is the head of a goddess protruding from the shell. The jug seems almost a stone-age prototype for Botticelli's "Birth of Venus." But in this case the scallop serves the goddess not as a boat but rather as her actual parent! The fact is that the Indians revered the scallop as the creature from whom Chalchiuhtlicue was reborn every full moon. They said that just as the ocean itself is constantly renewed by fresh water, so the sea-goddess renews herself in and with the scallop, at the height of the full-moon tide. This explains another Indian custom, which was to bury scallop shells with their dead. The shells in the tombs betokened rebirth, not of water but the spirit.

As the stone age gave way to the succeeding age of bronze, the sea-goddess grew ever more powerful, and the scallop waxed mightier along with her. Two thousand years before the time of Christ, the Minoans of Crete ruled the Mediterranean. On every shore of that sunlit sea they worshipped the "Great Sea-Mother." Her skirt was of the blue sea waves, serpents reared from her outstretched hands, and her breasts were swelling ivory with nipples of gold. Her sanctuaries were paved with scallop shells. All life sprang from her. And in due season everything returned to the Great Sea-Mother, who was in the beginning. In the beginning, the Cretans explained, she rose from the primordial scallop and danced upon the sea-waves, treading them out as she lifted up the sky. Then a cold coiling wind sprang up behind her, like a serpent following after, and she turned to dancing with the serpent, embracing him. After that she became a dove brooding upon the waters and laid a silver egg in the nest of darkness. This was the first full moon, whence came everything else that we know.

The Greeks brought in the age of iron, supplanted the Cretans as masters of the Mediterranean, and retired the Great Sea-Mother for a more consistently lovely and sportive divinity. According to some accounts, Aphrodite also was born from a scallop. A Greek jug made four centuries before the time of Christ bears a startling resemblance to the Peruvian version. This too has Aphrodite's head and shoulders emerging from the scallop, garlanded with pearls. One of her chief temples stood at Corinth, a wide-open sailors' town. Pirates and conquerors beached there with booty for the goddess: beautiful girls kidnapped on distant shores to be her temple harlots. Once an Olympic victor fulfilled a vow to Aphrodite by dedicating "one hundred limbs" at Corinth. That meant twenty-five girls. Corinth was a scandal to many Greeks but a must for thrill-seeking pilgrims. The Romans had a glum little saying about it: "Not everybody gets to Corinth." Yet whole armies of Romans did get to Corinth eventually. They besieged it, sacked it, occupied it and conquered Greece from it. They appropriated Aphrodite too, renaming her Venus, the laughter-loving. She became a dimpled beauty, appropriately bare, seated in a rose-covered chariot drawn by turtledoves. Not even the chariot of Venus, however, flew high enough to escape the onrushing tide: Christianity, which engulfed all the pagan gods together. However, the scallop, her ancient and half-forgotten consort, was destined to ride this new tide heaven-high. Freed of his old sea duties, born again, he would serve Christ, the saints and all mankind, as a regenerating power.

The first two apostles whom Jesus called were fishermen, Peter and James. When they set forth to "teach all nations," James undertook the conversion of cruel Spain, where the cold Ebro flows. Spain proved totally unreceptive. Finally James returned in defeat to Jerusalem, and there he was martyred. Yet what seemed the end of the story was really its beginning. His disciples rescued the saint's remains and conveyed them back again to Spain by ship. As the vessel approached the Spanish coast, a certain noble warrior was inspired to spur straight into the sea and welcome it. The man would certainly have drowned together with his horse, heavily armored as they were, had not a host of scallop appeared to buoy them along over the waves. Thereafter the body of James was said to work miracle upon miracle: the killing of a dragon, the taming of wild bulls, even the inundation of a hostile army. Thus James accomplished in death all that he had failed to do while living, and Spain became the cradle of Christian chivalry. The father of its knighthood, naturally, was the warrior saved by scallops. His brave plunge into the sea had been his baptism. And that is one reason why baptismal fonts are apt to be scallop-shaped, even today.

The final resting place of James remained a secret until eight hundred years after his death. It was revealed to a hermit in a vision of a particular meadow starred with wildflowers. The meadow lay in the Spanish kingdom of Galicia on the Bay of Biscay. And there the tomb was found. Soon a cathedral arose above the site and a town grew up around it called Santiago de Campostella, or "Saint James of the Starry Field." Medieval Europe flocked to it on pilgrimage. For centuries not even Rome had so many visitors in search of grace. The custom was for each pilgrim to come away from Santiago with a scallop shell signifying his own regeneration and thanks. Nobles proudly incorporated their shells in the family coat of arms, which helps to explain the existence of no fewer than nine hundred such arms in England alone. But ordinary pilgrims simply sewed the shells to their hat-brims, or else to the little satchels they used in lieu of pockets. Christ himself, they maintained, had carried a scallop shell. This is reasserted in Gothic art: the cloisters at Arles in France and at Silos in Spain both possess carvings of Christ with a scallop shell. In each case he is on the road to Emmaus, and the scallop attests his recent resurrection from the dead.

The starry pavements of the medieval world gave way at last before a new upwelling: the Renaissance. But artists and scholars still understood the scallop's significance. Practically all the Renaissance masters gave him an honored place in their art. If Botticelli's "Venus" carries the sweet tang of springtime on salt water, Piero della Francesca's "Blessed Virgin" sings of a world beyond our farthest seas. His Virgin stands before a scallop-shaped alcove from which hangs a shining egg. Great art will always elude categorical explanation. Suffice it to say that in the Renaissance the scallop came to symbolize a whole crescendo of pagan and Christian experience: birth, baptism, purity, fruitfulness and resurrection. Human hope, in a word.

But symbols are not the same as objects of belief. In time the force drains out of them and they lie inert, the province of specialists or the hobby of a few inquirers. Later they sink to the status of mere riddles in intellectual games. Finally they are forgotten, or remembered only in dreams. This is just what has happened in the scallop's case. His old-time tugging at the heartstrings of mankind seems to have ceased. And yet . . . all down the ages he has been reborn!

Versatile, serviceable, civilizing, self-renewing, hope-giving: such is the scallop. And such is his native element. We can learn from him and also from the lovely waters of the world. In a wild part of Cyprus is a spring which the Venetians called *Fontana Amorosa*—the Fountain of Love. Whoever bathes here must fall in love, they say. But this is not the dwelling place of a mischievous wood nymph merely, as the Italians thought. It is Aphrodite's spring. Here the love goddess used to bathe and renew her virginity. And still the clear water welcomes an occasional pilgrim. The water is soft and light, quicksilvery. Strangely, it does not feel wet. Or at least no more so than the touch of a lover's hand under water. One is floating within a wide grotto. The mossy, dripping rocks seem to waver in the rippling light. A gentle forest surrounds one, rich in underbrush and small birds. At the edge of the spring are blackberry bushes, the guards and nourishers of love. Half rising from the water, one plucks and eats. The air is sweet with oleander, myrtle and frascomili. Also there is a tang of purple grapes, very faint, and round about one senses the swaying pointed shadows of bamboo. The sky is half-mineral and half-vegetable, for an enormous fig tree comes out of the cliff and embraces the whole grotto.

The tree is the size of a small temple, with elephant-gray roots stepping down through the water into the rock crevices. Pure cool water runs and drips and splashes amidst the gray roots in the dusky shade of leaves massed layer upon layer overhead. The tree veils the grotto just as one of its leaves clothed our mother Eve, upon a time. The figs are tiny and inedible. Not as if this were the fig tree which Christ cursed, but simply because it is so very ancient and because it offers another kind of food. In the cool of the air, the moving shadows, here is some other nourishment, like motes of sunlight in shadow reflected from the moving water.

EPILOGUE

I HAD THOUGHT my book was done, and I walked over the mountain, like some thirsty bear, to celebrate. Well after midnight I started home again along the ridge. This was January, cold but very clear. The stars rained down their incandescent spears in sharply patterned salvos upon Mount Pentelikon and me. Staggering a little with my face uplifted, rapt in the ringing of a dark-silver gong, I felt the winds of legend sweep between my ribs, and the fires of yearning and the tongues of dread.

On such a night the snowy-maned god of the Norsemen gave

an eye for wisdom, for the red-gold ring which dripped and dripped a multitude of jewels resembling itself.

It was a night like this when Uchdryd Crossbeard flung the bristling red beard he had on him across the fifty rafters in King Arthur's hall.

Mankind has almost been destroyed many times, so they say. When by flood, the mountaineers survived. When by fire, it was the fishermen who put to sea and lived on. And on, under the incalculable immediacy of stars. But drunk as I was with resinated wine and the legendary wind and the starlight, I wanted all these things to be and happen as it were together. Had I toppled over a cliff at that moment it might have seemed natural.

Since that didn't happen, my heart began howling for fire in fire, love in wine. I almost expected a mountain dryad to reach out and call to me from the braided shadow of a silvery pine, to draw me down amongst the roots and mosses, the jeweled webs, the hair ferns and the wet light of crystals sprouting tight in rosy quartz.

Yet fire in itself is unlike any desire or dread either. Fire can be far and near, burning and freezing both at once, on such a night.

Reaching home at last, I lit the fire of myrtle roots and pine cones on the hearth. It spat sparks at me like a puppy dragon. With my fingers I absently combed the smoke from its yellow scales. Tonight I would not sleep at all; some turmoil was in me . . . I watched the flames search out the larger myrtle roots.

When the roots crumbled, at their hottest, I added a heavy chunk of olive wood. Its fragrance, suddenly released by the fire, brought back the olive groves of Crete. And this in turn conjured up an image of her far-wandering son, El Greco, with his smoky pointed beard. El Greco was not only a painter: he produced five books of philosophy. These were handwritten on heavy parchment, bound, and bequeathed to his son. They soon vanished. Fireworks were all the rage those days. Parchment came in handy for pinwheel casings, rocket caps and Roman candles. So perhaps El Greco's writings passed through some pyrotechnician's blackened hands. They would have made a six-minute tracery of clear-popping colors upon a night like this.

Jehovah, from a burning bush, commanded Moses to liberate his people. Long afterwards the Angel Gabriel, winged with glittering air, spoke joyfully to Mary and was gone, all in one great snowy rush. There had been a dove with him, a softer yet still brighter gleaming in the midst of all that whiteness. This scene El Greco painted many times, with a difference drawn from the Old Testament. He placed a branch in a vase at Mary's bedside, and set each twig alight. In his last "Annunciation" he tremendously enlarged this burning bush and let its light leap, leap like a poured-out pitcher of stars.

El Greco's paintings are tumultuous, and yet remembering them always calms me down. After a while I went to get a drink of water and look east from our back step. Amid the pines the marble boulders gleamed, one by one, as dawn broke like an ocean wave across the mountainside.

The world is revelation: open secrets. So are the Earth, Air, Fire and Water. These things are in us and we are in them. No lock, no door, bars the flowing of dawn into the world, the world into dawn. No door, no lock, bars the flowing of thought into the world, the world into thought. All is open to us and to the world. We children of night take joy in the coming of day. And as children of day we await the darkness again. Mysteries are flowing swift as dawn and starlight all about us, deep as breath and blood in us, pure as the clear, star-sparkling dawn.

The last stars vanished as I stood; they vanished but they did not close nor take their light away. Above the day tide they were shining still, like the flowers of the still dark mountain, elfin banners, emblazoned with an astral heraldry.

The world seems one thing at last. All experience partakes of this one thing. Science, scholarship, religion, philosophy and art play into the world, like minnows in the ocean.

Life and death are the ocean; what else is there? Something more, that swims by itself.

ABOUT THE AUTHOR

ALEXANDER ELIOT *belongs in the great tradition of Emerson and Thoreau, of nonsystematized New England writers and philosophers. A native of Cambridge, Massachusetts, he belongs in that tradition by birth as well. His great-grandfather was Charles W. Eliot, President of Harvard and editor of the "Five-Foot Shelf"; his grandfather was a Boston divine and President of the Unitarian Association; his father, a classical scholar, is Professor Emeritus of Drama at Smith College; his mother, Ethel Cook Eliot, is the author of a number of distinguished children's stories and Catholic novels.*

JANE WINSLOW ELIOT *was born in upper New York State and educated in this country as well as abroad. Her photographs, including the one of her husband on the jacket, were taken especially for this book.*

DATE DUE

DATE DUE			
MAR 8 '68			
NOV 1 6 1973			
GAYLORD			PRINTED IN U.S.A.

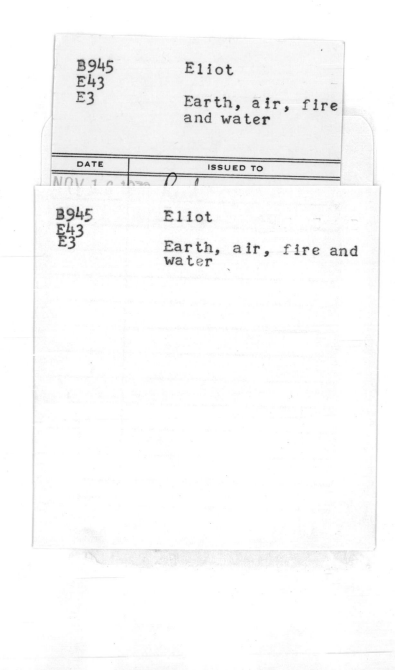

B945
E43
E3

Eliot

Earth, air, fire
and water

DATE	ISSUED TO

NOV 1 0 1939

B945
E43
E3

Eliot

Earth, air, fire and
water

ILLYRIS

MACEDONIA

Thessalonica

ADRIATIC SEA

ITALY

EPIRUS

Mt. Olympus

THRA

Dodona

THESSALY

ACARNANIA

Achelous River

EUBO

Thermopylae

LOCRIS

Mt. Parnassus

Myonia

Delphi

PHOCIS

Thebes

Mt. Helikon

BOEOTIA

Maru

ATTI

MEDITERRANEAN

ITHACA

GULF OF CORINTH

Eleusis

PI

SALA

ACHAIA

Corinth

ELIS

Erymanthos Mts.

ARGOLIS

Nemea

Olympia

ARCADIA

Mycenae

Epidaurus

IONIAN SEA

Argos

Tiryns

Alpheus R.

Lerna
(Miloi)

MESSENIA

MYR

SEA

Sparta

S

LACONIA

Cape
Malea

CYTHER

Ancient Greece